Palgrave Studies in Gender and Education

Series editor
Yvette Taylor
School of Education
University of Strathclyde
Glasgow, UK

This Series aims to provide a comprehensive space for an increasingly diverse and complex area of interdisciplinary social science research: gender and education. Because the field of women and gender studies is developing rapidly and becoming 'internationalised' – as are traditional social science disciplines such as sociology, educational studies, social geography, and so on – there is a greater need for this dynamic, global Series that plots emerging definitions and debates and monitors critical complexities of gender and education. This Series has an explicitly feminist approach and orientation and attends to key theoretical and methodological debates, ensuring a continued conversation and relevance within the well-established, inter-disciplinary field of gender and education. The Series combines renewed and revitalised feminist research methods and theories with emergent and salient public policy issues. These include pre-compulsory and post-compulsory education; 'early years' and 'lifelong' education; educational (dis)engagements of pupils, students and staff; trajectories and intersectional inequalities including race, class, sexuality, age and disability; policy and practice across educational landscapes; diversity and difference, including institutional (schools, colleges, universities), locational and embodied (in 'teacher'–'learner' positions); varied global activism in and beyond the classroom and the 'public university'; educational technologies and transitions and the (ir)relevance of (in)formal educational settings; and emergent educational mainstreams and margins. In using a critical approach to gender and education, the Series recognises the importance of probing beyond the boundaries of specific territorial-legislative domains in order to develop a more international, intersectional focus. In addressing varied conceptual and methodological questions, the Series combines an intersectional focus on competing – and sometimes colliding – strands of educational provisioning and equality and 'diversity', and provides insightful reflections on the continuing critical shift of gender and feminism within (and beyond) the academy.

More information about this series at
http://www.palgrave.com/series/14626

Gail Crimmins

Theatricalising Narrative Research on Women Casual Academics

palgrave
macmillan

Gail Crimmins
School of Communication and Creative Industries
University of the Sunshine Coast
Maroochydore, QLD, Australia

Palgrave Studies in Gender and Education
ISBN 978-3-319-71561-2   ISBN 978-3-319-71562-9   (eBook)
https://doi.org/10.1007/978-3-319-71562-9

Library of Congress Control Number: 2017960958

This Palgrave Macmillan imprint is published by Springer Nature
The registered company is Springer International Publishing AG
The registered company address is: Gewerbestrasse 11, 6330 Cham, Switzerland

'Arts based research at its best: Provocative, political, potent! Causal academics now account for huge numbers of faculty at many universities and within this group women far outnumber men. This breathtaking book offers uplifting and evocative narrative accounts of women's experiences in these roles. Through artful provocations Gail Crimmins skillfully engages narrative forms that are at once scholarly, playful, expressive and alternative as they offer important reconsiderations not only for women, but for all scholars pushing the boundaries of the academy.'
—Rita L. Irwin, *Distinguished University Scholar and Professor, Art Education, The University of British Columbia, Canada*

'Gail Crimmins weaves an evocative tapestry of scholarship from a wide range of disciplines to provide a backstage account of her intriguing arts-based project. Her proto-verbatim script and production are quality exemplars of research-informed theatre with a social justice agenda. Crimmins elevates qualitative inquiry by accomplishing one of its most deceptively complex goals: telling a good story that keeps its readers engaged. *Theatricalising Narrative Research On Women Casual Academics* is a significant contribution to the ethnotheatrical literature.'
—Johnny Saldaña, *Professor Emeritus of Theatre, Arizona State University, USA*

'Gail Crimmins brilliantly explodes the myth of meritocracy in the academy by sharing through story and image the lives of six women casual academics. Based on her doctoral arts informed research she weaves a tapestry of usually silenced voices and lived experiences (including her own) to explore: why it may take nearly 120 years to achieve equity in academe; the rise of casualised labour within universities; and, how feminine relational communication can address some of the polarities and tensions always present in higher education. This book not only celebrates the courage and resilience of women casual academics, it confronts us with the present untenable situation in academe and offers a way forward.'
—Robyn Ewing, *Professor of Teacher Education and the Arts, University of Sydney, Australia*

'This is an important and timely book that arrives at a moment when the academy is forced, perhaps more than ever before, to examine its core values. Gail Crimmins not only puts a vital and neglected item very firmly on to the agenda, she has done so through a highly original and engaging set of methodologies which themselves are part of a process for questioning some outdated hierarchies at the heart of university life. Whilst this should be read, of course, by senior academics and HR

departments, it would also be refreshing if copies found their way on to the desks of politicians who are interested in what is really happening inside universities.'
—Steve Blandford, *Emeritus Professor of Theatre, Film and Television, University of South Wales, UK*

'This important book provides a gripping account of real women's work experiences in the contemporary academy. A strength of the volume is the way Gail Crimmins makes these untold stories of workplace practice so vivid, through the theatricalising research and narrative process. A must read for anyone who employs casual staff, or who works as a casual academic.'
—Donna Lee Brien, *Professor, Creative Industries, CQUniversity, Australia*

'This is an important book that breaks new ground, highlighting not only the economic and social but also the emotional challenges of women casual academics.'
—Jeri Kroll, *Professor Emeritus, Flinders University, Australia*

'In this incredibly insightful and moving book, researcher-scholartist Gail Crimmins presents a deeply troubling re-storying of the lived experiences of women casual academics in Australian universities. In *Theatricalising Narrative Research on Women Casual Academics*, Gail Crimmins not only makes a significant contribution to the fields of higher education and feminist research but also illustrates new ways of combining the arts and narrative inquiry from which a new polyvocal, dialogic form of arts-informed research emerges. This book reveals how new forms of communication can inspire, provoke, and stimulate new conversations within academia and create new forms of academic research. This is a must read for those on courses in feminism and feminist theory, gender and women's studies, narrative inquiry and arts-based research methodology at all levels and a mandatory reading for higher education leaders and management.'
—Pamela Burnard, *Professor of Arts, Creativities and Education, University of Cambridge, UK*

*This book is dedicated to women casual academics
keeping the academy afloat,
drowning, not waving*

FOREWORD

Gail Crimmins brings to this volume an eclectic wealth of multidisciplinary experiences. Her background in theatre certainly enabled her to create a well scripted and – more important – well performed ethnotheatrical production. The accompanying YouTube videos of the performance are a high-quality exemplar of what the genre can accomplish. But Crimmins offers her readers so much more than just the documentation of a research-informed, arts-based project.

Dr. Crimmins masterfully and intricately weaves selected literature from higher education, feminist theory, narrative inquiry, autoethnography, poetic inquiry, aesthetics, dramatic theory and criticism, philosophy, ethics, and other fields into a thoughtful and evocative treatise. She presents herself with humble vulnerability as she reveals her deep reflexivity on the part-time employment dilemmas of women in academia, as well as the potential of art itself as an instrument for social justice. Crimmins elevates arts-based qualitative inquiry by accomplishing one of its most deceptively complex goals: telling a good story that keeps its readers engaged.

Theatricalising Narrative Research on Women Casual Academics is an important contribution to the ethnodramatic and ethnotheatrical literature. It is a rare, backstage account of how a research-informed production evolved, from conception to post-performance evaluation. The women's stories Crimmins adapted and staged are elegantly written, retold honestly and believably by a company of professional performers. This book is a significant model for how rigorous scholarship can lead to the creation of research work with artistic rigor.

Professor Emeritus of Theatre   Johnny Saldaña
Arizona State University, USA

PROLOGUE

Welcome to the prologue to a backstage account of theatricalising narrative research on Women Casual Academics. Its main function is to introduce myself to you, and to acknowledge that I – to a certain extent – am entering your life, if even for the short time it takes for you to read these words. We are hereby forming a research relationship and so it would be ridiculous to pretend that 'I', and 'we' as people and co-constructors of meaning, don't exist. I therefore introduce myself to you:

I was born in Cardiff, South Wales, into a 'proud-to-be-working-class' family of four. My mum was a support nurse in an aged care facility – though we called them old people's homes back then – and my father was a labourer in the building and heavy industries. My mum 'worked nights' so she could take us and collect us from school and 'do tea' (a colloquialism, I was later to discover, for preparing dinner). My dad worked when and where he could, often working 'a doubler' (which means working back to back shifts of 6 am–2 pm, and 2 pm–10 pm, of hard physical labour). The coal and steel industries which were the economic backbone of South Wales were being closed down and I grew up at a time of high unemployment, so you took whatever work you could, whenever you could get it. It was also a time of political activism and the feminist movement was in full swing; I remember my mum wearing a badge that read, 'A woman needs a man like a fish needs a bicycle'. We laughed.

At school, a local comprehensive, I was an average student academically, but enjoyed hanging out with friends, netball, and Drama. When I was 14 years old my then drama teacher – Janet Free – wrote on my report card that 'Gail has an excellent flair for Drama'. This comment, quote short and simple, was life-changing. I had never before excelled, or rather, had never before been told I was excellent at anything. I continued to enjoy in Drama, buoyed by the sense that I had some talent for it, and went on to study it at university. I loved it. My undergraduate course offered a practical drama training and we performed, 'showed' and 'shared' our work regularly, but were only required to create two short written pieces of work throughout the 3-year program. I therefore became a confident and competent performer but was intimated by written communication. I could communicate clearly and with ease in my colloquial South Wales dialect and through character in physical and vocal performance, but neither of these languages seemed to resemble 'university writing'. Indeed, Professor Peter Thomson, a highly respected theatre scholar and my teacher and friend, wrote at the bottom of my first piece of writing: 'Very good understandings of character and plot, but you tend to write wearing your Sunday best'. This was another comment that stayed/stays with me.

The reason I wrote 'wearing my Sunday best', I realise now, was that I thought that the only form of communication that was acceptable in academia was the formal, terse, 'objective' form of traditional discourse I encountered when reading academic literature. I thus adopted a persona, with a middle-class accent/code of academic respectability and convention – complete with dress code – to write 'academically'. I didn't trust that I could write as myself and still be heard, understood, or taken seriously. I distinguished, probably unconsciously, between the words and expressions I use/d in my daily life, and the communication I use/d on paper.

This discursive separation continued until fairly recently. However, in the process of researching and re-presenting the lived experience of women casual academics, a journey that informs this book, I encountered the writings of Cixous (1986, 1998), Richardson (1997, 1999, 2000, 2001), Childers et al. (2013) and MacLure (2013) – writers who advocated and demonstrated a freedom in writing, writing as a creative process, and as self-expression. The literature with which I engaged prompted me to reconceptualise *who* could write, and *how* we might write, and I slowly began the process of 'de-disciplining' my writing (Richardson 1997), in order to *re*-discipline it. In this book, I therefore employ a bicultural form of communication (Blankenship and Robson 1995), a form which merges traditional discourse of logically developed premises and academic citation with feminine with first person, reflective communication.

This book thus reflects my growing confidence in using language and image to express my personal account of undertaking an arts informed research process and unearthing and re-presenting the lived experience of women casual academics.

This short story of my 'background' is presented here to explain why I use the forms of communication I do, and to invite you to also use the form/s of eloquence with which you are gifted (whether that's painting, performance, prose, poetry, or song). Speak in your tongue as your truths are as worthy as those (of the tailored pin-stripes) of established writers.

To You

I also write this prologue to acknowledge you – you, reading this in snippets or in chapters, in pyjamas or in 'work clothes', on the train or on the run, hungry or full, in the spring or the fall. You are my fellow meaning maker/s and I do not pretend that you don't exist, that somehow this text is created and engaged with by no-bodies. Indeed, as you dip in and out of the following chapters you will make sense of the words and images I share, and some words, white space, images and videos will be more meaningful to you than others. I'd like to welcome you therefore, and *thank you* for taking the time to engage, ponder, consider, feel, and think your way through this work.

Against the Grain

Thank you for choosing to open this book
for wondering what it feels like, sounds like, and looks like to be a woman casual academic,
or for being curious about the process of unearthing stories through a narrative inquiry,
and for pondering the process of consciously re-constructing stories so that they compel us to engage.

Your wonderings go against the academic grain
where the dominant discourse of Higher Education is one of ~~masculinity~~ meritocracy
where statistics hold sway in the hierarchy of knowledge,
and where information is presented to appeal to logic, only.

I stand with you 'against-the-grainers'. In this work, I seek to expose the myth of meritocracy in the academy, I too understand and 'feel' that stories represent peoples' knowledges and truths and as such deserve representation, and I share with you the desire to find forms of communication that compel our fully embodied selves to listen and care for Others' experience.

REFERENCES

Blankenship, J., & Robson, D. C. (1995). A "Feminine Style"; in Women's Political Discourse: An Exploratory Essay. *Communication Quarterly, 43*(3), 353–366. https://doi.org/10.1080/01463379509369982

Childers, S. M., Rhee, J.-E., & Daza, S. L. (2013). Promiscuous (Use of) Feminist Methodologies: The Dirty Theory and Messy Practice of Educational Research Beyond Gender. *International Journal of Qualitative Studies in Education, 26*(5), 507–523. https://doi.org/10.1080/09518398.2013.786849

Cixous, H. (1998). *Stigmata: Escaping Texts.* London: Routledge.

Cixous, H., & Clément, C. (1986). *The Newly Born Woman* (trans: Wing, B.). Minneapolis: University of Minnesota Press.

MacLure, M. (2013). The Wonder of Data. *Cultural Studies↔ Critical Methodologies, 13*(4), 228–232. https://doi.org/10.1177/1532708613487863

Richardson, L. (1997). Skirting a Pleated Text: De-Disciplining an Academic Life. *Qualitative Inquiry, 3*(3), 295–303. https://doi.org/10.1177/107780049700300303

Richardson, L. (1999). Feathers in Our Cap. *Journal of Contemporary Ethnography, 28*(6), 660–668. https://doi.org/10.1177/089124199129023767

Richardson, L. (2000). Writing: A Method of Inquiry. In N. K. Denzin & Y. S. Lincoln (Ed.), *Handbook of Qualitative Research,* (pp. 923–948). Thousand Oaks: Sage.

Richardson, L. (2001). Getting Personal: Writing-Stories. *International Journal of Qualitative Studies in Education, 14*(1), 33–38. https://doi.org/10.1080/09518390010007647

ACKNOWLEDGEMENT

I would very much like to acknowledge and offer sincerest gratitude to the women casual academics whose stories inspired this book, and thank Drs Bill Allen and Sue Simon whose intellect, creativity and humanity guided the research journey I share with you here.

To a wonderful cast – Sharon Grimley, Anna McMahon, Rainee Skinner, Lyn Stevenson and Natasha (Tasha) Tidey-Stevens, and fabulous crew – Dave Blake, Tahlia Kertesz and Lara Qualtrough, who gifted this project with both their talent and a generosity of spirit, I am forever humbled by your gifts. Thank you.

I sincerely thank and acknowledge the skills and artistry of Kath Ogle and Kristel Blair for their photography and art works which help to bring to life/imagination the lived experience of women casual academics.

I acknowledge also Kristel Alla and the editorial team at Palgrave, especially Eleanor Christie and Becky Wyde, for their patience, and for encouraging and supporting this book.

Finally, I thank my parents for bringing me up to understand that the moon belongs to everyone, and that not to act/not to speak, is itself a political act; and to Dave, Eadie and William – the loves of my life – my deepest thanks go to you for giving me the confidence and freedom to write this book.

And I'd choose you; in a hundred lifetimes,
in a hundred worlds,
in any version of reality,
I'd find you and I'd choose you. (Kiersten White, 2013)

CONTENTS

1 The Silence of Women Casual Academics in Australian
  Universities   1

2 The Limitations of Traditional Academic Conventions
  and an Embrace of Imagistic Communication   13

3 Orienting My Map to North   27

4 The Philosophical, Ethical and Political Considerations
  Involved in Theatricalising Data   45

5 The Plays the Thing Wherein I'll Capture
  the Consciousness of an Audience   63

6 A Personal Process of Restorying Lived Experience
  into a Proto-Verbatim Performance   81

7 A Re-view of the Process and Impact of Theatricalising
  Narrative Research on Women Casual Academics   101

Index   117

LIST OF FIGURES

Fig. 1.1	Weight of (heavy) heart	5
Fig. 4.1	Refractions	48
Fig. 6.1	Every woman has a story	86
Fig. 6.2	They only do it because they can't get a job doing anything else	87
Fig. 6.3	I can't plan	87
Fig. 6.4	A relentless and underpaid work experience	90
Fig. 6.5	Hopeful	92
Fig. 6.6	Jilted	92
Fig. 6.7	You can't speak up	93
Fig. 6.8	Often it's very frightening	94
Fig. 7.1	Theatricalising narrative research on women casual academics	102

CHAPTER 1

The Silence of Women Casual Academics in Australian Universities

Abstract This chapter exposes the voicelessness of women casual academics within Higher Education. It also establishes how a lack of contribution by women casual academics to academic scholarship serves to perpetuate the myth of meritocracy within Higher Education; privileges the already advantaged masculine voice; and limits the celebration of a multiplicity of stories, storytellers, and story forms within the academy. The story woven through this chapter therefore offers a compelling rationale for developing an Arts-based narrative inquiry into the lived experience of women casual academics. This chapter also introduces the bicultural form of communication with which the book weaves its research story where language is used to evoke affect as well as carry meaning.

Keywords Casual academics • Gender in higher education • Masculine discourse • Voice

In this short contextualising chapter, I explain my reasoning and reflect on my emotional compulsion to unearth and share the stories of women casual academics in Australian universities. In particular, I discuss how, despite increases in the numbers of women in higher education over the last 40 years, they predominantly furnish lower academic staffing positions, and that it is likely to take 119 years for women to achieve equity in

© The Author(s) 2018   1
G. Crimmins, *Theatricalising Narrative Research on Women Casual Academics*, Palgrave Studies in Gender and Education, https://doi.org/10.1007/978-3-319-71562-9_1

the professoriate. Relatedly, I consider that a lack of contribution by women casual academics to academic scholarship can serve to privilege the already advantaged masculine academic voice and concerns, and limit the celebration of a multiplicity of stories, storytellers, and story forms. This phenomenon, if left unchallenged, not only marginalises women in academia, but it stultifies the breadth and depth of what – and how – academia can explore and achieve.

The chapter therefore establishes the platform to harness stories that celebrate the courage and persistence of women causal academics.

THE ELEPHANT/S IN THE ROOM

There is an elephant in the room of academia
It's a rather significant elephant
As elephants go it's pretty impressive
The elephant is the casualisation of academia

And she's not alone
Academia has quite a few of these large and imposing mammals
A second, sister/mother elephant, is the gendered stratification of contemporary academia
Let's not pretend they don't exist
Let's name/shame them.

The largest contingency of academic staff in Australian and American universities are casual academics where 61% of academic staff in Australian universities and 70% of faculty teaching positions in the non-profit higher education sector in America are employed on what are described as casual contracts (Kezar and Maxey 2015; May et al. 2011). Similarly, more than 50% of university teaching is undertaken by casual academics in the UK, France, Germany and Japan (Bryson 2013), who are women (May et al. 2011; Rea 2012).

In addition, most casual academics are women, and the gendered nature of casualisations sits within an equally gendered stratification of academic employment. For, while the overall trend over the last 40 years has been an increase in the number of women in higher education (both as students and staff) in most countries, their presence in the senior and executive level positions remains disproportionately low (Machado-Taylor et al. 2008). For instance, despite the fact that women make up over 50% of graduates in Europe, the US and Australia, only 21% of full professors are women in Europe (European Commission 2016), 24% of professors in the US are women (Monroe et al. 2014), and less than a third of women academics in Australia are promoted to above Senior Lecturer, compared to 69% of men (Grieshaber 2016; Vernos 2013). Indeed, at the current rate of recruitment and promotion it will take 119 years for women to achieve equal numbers in the professoriate (Acker et al. 2016).

I gasp.

At the current rate of recruitment and promotion it will take 119 years for women to achieve equal numbers in the professoriate (Acker et al. 2016).
  These statistics shock and sadden me.
  I have a ten-year-old daughter, Eadie. Eadie and I talk about equal opportunities and affordances often, but with current rates of recruitment and promotions it is likely to take the birth of Eadie's daughter's daughter's daughter (if this becomes a reality) before equal gender representation will exist in the academy. This reflects both a waste of women's talent and ingenuity, and a discriminatory cruelty.
  In addition, leaning into Lorde's (2012) notion that there is no such thing as a single issue and we do not live single-issue lives, international data that demonstrates how women in academia are generally more likely than men to enter casual, fixed-period, short-term, part-time *and* contractual agreements (or precarious contractual arrangements), also upsets me. In particular, in the UK permanent full-time contracts were held by 61% of men compared to 39% women (Higher Education Statistics Agency 2017), and in the European Union the rates of researchers engaged in part-time work in 2012 was 9% for men and 32% for women (European Commission 2016). Similarly, Curtis (2011) established that despite the general trend in the last 40 years for both genders to be increasingly employed on a part-time basis across the US higher education institutions, the higher proportion of women in part-time employment has persisted. Concomitantly, precarious employment was lower for men than for women in the academy. In particular, in the US women have consistently been found to be more disadvantaged in terms of tenure, where a study of 106 cases of junior faculty at a US university found that as many as 92% of male academics were offered tenure compared to only 55% of women (Junn 2012). In Australia, while comprehensive public data is lacking (Andrews et al. 2016), individual studies have confirmed that the majority

of academic staff who identify themselves as casual academics in Australia are women (Brown et al. 2013; Coates and Goedegebuure 2010).

Relatedly, there appears to be a persistent gender gap in earnings that favours men in academia across the world to such a degree that the U.S. Department of Education (2016) sets the average salary for male academics at 21% above that for females (2014–15) and, data from the Higher Education Statistics Agency shows that in 2015–16, women in the UK received an annual pay that was about 12% less than male scholars (Higher Education Statistics Agency 2017). In the European Union more generally, in 2010 women academics had average gross hourly earnings that were 18% lower than for men. Canada and Australia mirror these gender imbalances in pay, as women academics in Canada receive 89% of the average salaries of their male colleagues (Canadian Association of University Teachers 2011), and Australian female academics earn around 83% of male weekly earnings (Bailey et al. 2016). Thus, Hearn's assertion that the academy is an 'incredibly hierarchical gendered institution' (Hearn 2001, 72) seems to be internationally borne out.

The Statistics Do Not Reveal the 'How' of Experience

However, even though this landscape of academic staffing is shocking, it only provides *background* to this study as percentages and numbers fail to detail or make known the 'how' of the lived experience of the casual academic. And the quantitative research instruments that are used to amass such data have been criticised for creating typologies that fail to humanise or individualise 'the researched'. Such measurements have also been described as an 'essentially masculine way of interpreting' experience' (Stanley and Wise 1983, 40). More specifically, there has been criticism that data derived from large-scale survey designed and disseminated by people outside of the casual academic experience (Brown 2010; Pocock et al. 2004) has been privileged over first-hand accounts of the actual experience. This privileging has meant that my human experience of being a female casual academics (the largest cohort of academic staff) was 'yet to be voiced' (Arnot and Reay 2007) and so remained unknown (Coates et al. 2009).

As an academic employed on short fixed term contracts (in the same academic role since 2012, at the point in writing that's five years) I live in a state of un-ease and lack any assurance that I will be employed next year. I am one of many. In fact, I am one of a majority minority in the contemporary academy.

I found, and still find, it an unfunny irony that women casual academics constitute the largest demography in most contemporary universities, yet our scholarship rarely finds print, and our stories are seldom heard outside the corridor conversations we may share with other casual academics. We are talked *about* 'in the literature', mainly as number or percentage. Yet we have our own stories to tell and our truths have arms, legs, voices and breath. Our experience cannot be contained in full points or fractions, they are bigger than spreadsheets. Our entireties and emergences don't fit into boxes and tables labelled 'age', 'highest qualification gained', 'number of years employed' (Fig. 1.1).

We are more than the sum of the parts so neatly compartmentalised and captioned in the story told about us.

Bhabha (1990) suggests that a nation shapes itself through the stories it tells about itself, then I feel that the stories of casualisation currently told

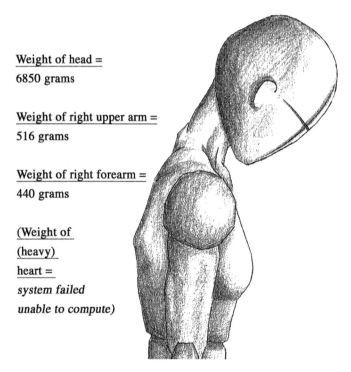

Weight of head =
6850 grams

Weight of right upper arm =
516 grams

Weight of right forearm =
440 grams

(Weight of
(heavy)
heart =
system failed
unable to compute)

Fig. 1.1   Weight of (heavy) heart

are recounted in weights and measures, and the shape of the narrative is
hollow and lacks guts. It sketches an outline but offers no texture of flesh.

Also, when academic discourse is generated and maintained by 'established', fully tenured academics the views and practices of established academics and academia are privileged. This is especially true when the voice
(in form and content) of 'Others' is not included (Lea and Street 1998).
This appears to be the case within the dominant discourses around casualisation of academic, where casual academics' only contribution is as anonymous respondents to pre-set research questions in large scale surveys
established from a privileged academic frame of reference. Consequently,
academic scholarship around casualisation perpetuates a discourse of academia that privileges the already privileged academic voice, consequently
rendering the casual academic voiceless.

Such a lack of voice of women casual academics in the existing discourses around casualisation is a problem because, as Belenky et al. (1986)
argued, women who are denied a voice in public discourse, who rely 'on
what others told them about themselves to get any sense of self' (Belenky
et al. 1986, 31) suffer the oppression of voicelessness. Additionally, a lack
of contribution by women casual academics to academic scholarship can
serve to perpetuate a narrative of academia that privileges the already privileged male academic voice, fails to make visible the gendered practice/
disadvantages in academic workplaces (Rindfleish et al. 2009; Strachan
et al. 2007), and prevents the celebration of a multiplicity of stories and
storytellers within academic organisations (Boje 1995).

As a result, Rindfleish et al. (2009) suggest that 'more stories need to
be heard in openly public spaces for there to be some recognition of the
ongoing disadvantage women experience in academia' (Rindfleish et al.
2009, 487). They also proposed that the presentation of women academics' stories in public places can resist the hegemony of privileged stories
of academia (Rindfleish et al. 2009). Similarly, Boje established the
importance of celebrating a multiplicity of stories and storytellers within
academic organisations (Boje 1995). Finally, this phenomenon (of voicelessness), if left unchallenged, not only marginalises women in academia,
but it stultifies the breadth and depth of what – and how – academia can
explore and achieve.

For these reasons, I was ~~persuaded~~ compelled to tell a different story of the
casualisation of academia, in a different voice and form.
Compelled?

Am I 'allowed' to feel compelled to act in academia?
Surely not!
Compulsion is full of emotional charge,
associated with desire,
that which is considered dichotomous to reason and logic
that which is dichotomous to academia.

But yes, it *was* my emotional response to how it *felt* to be a causal academic, rendered invisible in the accounts *about* casualisation, muted and made immobile by pie charts, that drew me to explore other women's lived experience of being casual academia. The scholarship around casualisations and gendered stratification cited above supported, reinforced and is used to 'validate' my investigation, but it didn't motivate it. It was instead what Adsit and her colleagues call the 'fatalistic feelings that accompany the recognition of oppressive working conditions' (2015, p.32) that stimulated my research. And for that I make no apology. In fact, by utilising my sadness/rage to spur my research sees me standing with Leys (2011) who identifies that emotions and affects have political potential. Likewise, Adsit et al. (2015) state that acting on the unhappiness caused by inequity disrupts a state of neutrality and challenges the 'emotional hegemony' 'that serves to maintain the status quo in naturalized power relations' (2015, 32). I thus also accept Cvetkovich's (2012) position that emotions needs be de-pathologised, reframed, but used instead to propel activism. In my case, my feelings of marginalisation, of not feeling 'good enough' for a permanent appointment, propelled me into unearthing Others' stories of the lived experience of women casual academics.

STORIES AS A WAY OF KNOWING AND COMMUNICATING

In contrast, and in conscious contestation, to the narrow measurement and statistical representation of millions of casual academics around the world, I felt compelled, physically and emotionally, to publicly communicate women casual academic's embodied stories. Stories and storying are understood in this work as both a way of knowing, and a way of communicating what we know or understand.

Theoretically, there is a strong, and relatively long traditional that supports how we come to know and communicate through stories. In fact, Barbara Hardy (1968) first established narrative as a primary act of the mind 50 years ago. She claimed that

we dream,
day-dream,
remember,
anticipate,
hope,
believe,
plan,
and learn, through narrative.

She also understood self-narration to be an essential part of our living and knowing: 'In order really to live, we make up stories about ourselves and others, about the personal as well as the social past and future. Indeed, Hardy claimed that narrative

lends imagination to the otherwise (Hardy 1968, 5–6).

I've allowed the white space around these worlds to allow you to ponder them, and to appreciate their eloquence. I sat with these words for a while when I first encountered them, allowing them to seep into my pours. For who could not wish to image the otherwise when we live/work in such a stratified and gendered environment?

Then, Jerome Bruner in 1986, 1990, and 1996 traversed beyond Hardy's understanding of the routine nature of narrative knowing when he suggested that there is a 'human readiness for narrative', and that we share a 'predisposition to organize experience into a narrative form, into plot structures' (1990, 45). Using psychological experiments Bruner demonstrated that humans automatically ascribe human characteristics, such as moving with intent to establish relationships and connection or self-protection, to non-human figures and shapes. In the experiments discussed by Bruner research participants consistently described the movement of the shapes narratively by constructing plots in which larger rectangular 'bullies' pursue smaller circles and triangles (1986, 17–19). As a result, Bruner claimed that man has a human orientation towards organising experience into narratives that incorporate character, intentions and plight.

Similarly, Barthes claimed that 'narrative is present at all times, in all places, in all societies; the history of narrative begins with the history of mankind; there does not exist, and never has existed, a people without narratives' (1966, 14) and Gare suggested that to know narratively is a primordial act employed 'in the creation of the self, and of culture, and in all social and intellectual life' (2007, 95).

Therefore, based on this understanding that we come to know and understand, and communicate our lives, through stories that employ characters, settings and plot lines; and motivated by wanting to address the current voicelessness and body-less-ness of women casual academics in the narratives/discourses of the academy, I sought to elicit the lived experience and stories of women casual academics. My aim was to acknowledge the lived experience of women causal academics by extending the existing academic discourses around casualisation to *include* the voice/s of women casual academics them/ourselves. And this book tells the story of how I attempted to do this.

Finally, I understand acknowledgement to mean 'what happens to knowledge… when it is sanctioned, when it is made part of the public scene' (Weschler 1990, 4). By making public the stories of women casual academics it was my hope that the experience and insights of women casual academics would become part of the public consciousness, and that their/our voice be heard.

So, to celebrate a multiplicity of stories, storytellers, and story forms in the academy, and to acknowledge the lived experience of women casual academies, I chose to harness and re-present stories that celebrate the courage and persistence of women causal academics and point to the elephant/s in the room (of academia). I will reflect on how I manoeuvre/d through this research within the following six chapters.

References

Acker, S., Webber, M., & Smyth, E. (2016). Continuity or Change? Gender, Family, and Academic Work for Junior Faculty in Ontario Universities. *NASPA Journal About Women in Higher Education, 9*(1), 1–20. https://doi.org/10.1 080/19407882.2015.1114954

Adsit, J., Doe, S., Allison, M., Maggio, P., & Maisto, M. (2015). Affective Activism: Answering Institutional Productions of Precarity in the Corporate University. *Feminist Formations, 27*(3), 21–48. https://doi.org/10.1353/ ff.2016.0008

Andrews, S., Bare, L., Bentley, P., Goedegebuure, L., Pugsley, C., & Rance, B. (2016). *Contingent Academic Employment in Australian Universities.* http:// www.lhmartininstitute.edu.au/documents/publications/2016-contingent-academic-employment-in-australian-universities-updatedapr16.pdf. Accessed 4 Sept 2017.

Arnot, M., & Reay, D. (2007). A Sociology of Pedagogic Voice: Power, Inequality and Pupil Consultation. *Discourse: Studies in the Cultural Politics of Education, 28*(3), 311–325. https://doi.org/10.1080/01596300701458814

Bailey, J., Peetz, D., Strachan, G., Whitehouse, G., & Broadbent, K. (2016). Academic Pay Loadings and Gender in Australian Universities. *Journal of Industrial Relations, 58*(5), 647–668. https://doi.org/10.1177/0022185616639308

Barthes, R. (1966). *Introduction to the Structural Analysis of Narrative*. Occasional Paper. Birmingham: Centre for Contemporary Cultural Studies, University of Birmingham.

Belenky, M. F., Clinchy, B. M., Goldberger, N. R., & Tarule, J. M. (1986). *Women's Ways of Knowing: The Development of Self, Voice and Mind*. New York: Basic Books.

Bhabha, H. K. (1990). *Nation and Narration*. London: Routledge.

Boje, D. M. (1995). Stories of the Storytelling Organization: A Postmodern Analysis of Disney as "Tamara-Land". *The Academy of Management Journal, 38*(4), 997–1035. https://doi.org/10.2307/256618

Brown, P. (2010). *Verbatim: Staging Memory and Community*. Sydney: Currency Press.

Brown, N. R., Kelder, J.-A., Freeman, B., & Carr, A. R. (2013). A Message from the Chalk Face – What Casual Teaching Staff Tell Us They Want to Know, Access and Experience *Journal of University Teaching & Learning Practice, 10*(3), 1–16. http://ro.uow.edu.au/jutlp/vol10/iss3/6

Bruner, J. S. (1986). *Actual Minds, Possible Worlds*. London: Harvard University Press.

Bruner, J. S. (1990). *Acts of Meaning*. Cambridge: Harvard University Press.

Bruner, J. S. (1996). *The Culture of Education*. Cambridge: Harvard University Press.

Bryson, C. (2013). Supporting Sessional Teaching Staff in the UK – To What Extent Is There Real Progress? *Journal of University Teaching and Learning Practice, 10*(3), 1–17. http://ro.uow.edu.au/julp/vol10/iss3/2

Canadian Association of University Teachers. (2011). The Persistent Gap: Understanding Male-Female Salary Differentials Amongst Canadian Academic Staff. *CAUT Equity Review*. https://www.caut.ca/sites/default/files/the-persistent-gap-mdash-understanding-male-female-salary-differentials-amongst-canadian-academic-staff-mar-2011.pdf. Accessed 2 Sept 2017.

Coates, H., & Goedegebuure, L. (2010). *The Real Academic Revolution: Why We Need to Reconceptualise Australia's Future Academic Workforce, and Eight Possible Strategies for How to Go About This*. Melbourne: LH Martin Institute for Higher Education Leadership and Management.

Coates, H., Dobson, I., Edwards, D., Friedman, T., Goedegebuure, L., & Meek, L. (2009). *The Attractiveness of the Australian Academic Profession: A Comparative Analysis*. Melbourne: University of Melbourne.

Curtis, J. W. (2011, April 11). *Persistent Inequity: Gender and Academic Employment*. Prepared for "New Voices in Pay Equity". An Event for Equal Pay Day. https://www.aaup.org/NR/rdonlyres/08E023AB-E6D8-4DBD-99A0-24E5EB73A760/0/persistent_inequity.pdf. Accessed 4 Sept 2017.

Cvetkovich, A. (2012). *Depression: A Public Feeling*. Durham: Duke University Press.

de Machado-Taylor, M. L., Carvalho, M. T., & White, K. (2008). *Women and Higher Education Leadership in Portugal and Australia*. Paper Presented at SRHE Conference, Liverpool.

European Commission. (2016). *SHE Figures 2015*. Luxembourg: Publications Office of the European Union.

Gare, A. (2007). The Primordial Role of Stories in Human Self-Creation. *Cosmos and history. The Journal of Natural and Social Philosophy, 3*(1), 93–114. http://cosmosandhistory.org/index.php/journal/article/viewFile/56/579

Grieshaber, S. (2016). *Women in the Professoriate and the Boys' Club in Australian Universities*. http://monash.edu/education/events/deans-lecture-series/sue-grieshaber.html. Accessed 6 Oct 2017.

Hardy, B. (1968). Towards a Poetics of Fiction: 3) an Approach Through Narrative. NOVEL: A Forum on Fiction, *2*(1), 5–14. https://doi.org/10.2307/1344792

Hearn, J. (2001). Academia, Management and Men: Making the Connections, Exploring the Implications. In A. Brooks & A. McKinnon (Eds.), *Gender and the Reconstructed University: Changing Management and Culture in Higher Education* (pp. 69–89). Buckingham: Open University Press.

Higher Education Statistics Agency. (2017). *Higher Education Statistics for the UK 2015/16*. https://www.hesa.ac.uk/data-and-analysis/publications/higher-education-2015-16. Accessed 17 Sept 2017.

Junn, J. (2012). *Analysis of Data on Tenure at USC Dornsife*. https://feministphilosophers.files.wordpress.com/2016/05/c9093-junnreport.pdf. Accessed 17 Sept 2017.

Kezar, A., & Maxey, D. (2015). *Adapting by Design: Creating Faculty Roles and Defining Faculty Work to Ensure an Intentional Future for Colleges and Universities*. http://www.thechangingfaculty.org/adaptingbydesign.html. Accessed 6 Oct 2017.

Lea, M. R., & Street, B. V. (1998). Student Writing in Higher Education: An Academic Literacies Approach. *Studies in Higher Education, 23*(2), 157–172. https://doi.org/10.1080/03075079812331380364

Leys, R. (2011). Affect and intention: A reply to William E. Connolly. *Critical Inquiry, 37*(4), 799–805.

Lorde, A. (2012). *Sister Outsider: Essays and Speeches*. New York: The Crossing Press.

May, R., Strachan, G., Kaye, B., & Peetz, D. (2011). The Casual Approach to University Teaching; Time for a Re-think? In K.-L. Krause, M. Buckridge, C. Grimmer, & S. Purbrick-Illeck (Eds.), *Research and Development in Higher*

Education: Reshaping Higher Education (Vol. 34). Gold Coast: Research and Development Society of Australasia, Inc.

Monroe, K. R., Choi, J., Howell, E., Lampros-Monroe, C., Trejo, C., & Perez, V. (2014). Gender Equality in the Ivory Tower, and How Best to Achieve It. *PS: Political Science & Politics, 47*(2), 418–426. https://doi.org/10.1017/S104909651400033X

Pocock, B., Buchanan, J., & Campbell, I. (2004). *Meeting the Challenge of Casual Work in Australia: Evidence, Past Treatment and Future Policy.* Sydney: Chifley Research Foundation.

Rea, J. (2012). *National Tertiary Education Union Written Submission to the Independent Inquiry to Insecure Work.* http://www.nteu.org.au/library/view/id/2186. Accessed 13 Nov 2013.

Rindfleish, J., Sheridan, A., & Kjeldal, S.-E. (2009). Creating an "Agora" for Storytelling as a Way of Challenging the Gendered Structures of Academia. *Equal Opportunities International, 28*(6), 486–499. https://doi.org/doi:10.1108/02610150910980783

Stanley, L., & Wise, S. (1983). *Breaking Out Again: Feminist Ontology and Epistemology.* London: Routledge.

Strachan, G., Burgess, J., & Henderson, L. (2007). Equal Employment Opportunity Legislation and Policies: The Australian Experience. *Equal Opportunities International, 26*(6), 525–540. https://doi.org/doi:10.1108/02610150710777024

U.S. Department of Education. (2016). *Digest of Education Statistics 2017, Table 315.20.* Washington, DC: Department of Education, National Center for Education Statistics.

Vernos, I. (2013). Research Management: Quotas Are Questionable. *Nature, 495*(7439), 39–39. https://doi.org/10.1038/495039a

Weschler, L. (1990). *A Miracle: A Universe.* New York: Pantheon.

CHAPTER 2

The Limitations of Traditional Academic Conventions and an Embrace of Imagistic Communication

Abstract This chapter discusses the pervasive nature and limitation of traditional forms of academic communication by reflecting on how scientific, impersonal language in highly structured forms can alienate researchers from their personhoods, from the people they study and write about, and from the readers of academic research. It also ponders the myth of neutral research representation, and suggests that feminine forms of communication can offer a more inclusive and expressive alternative to traditional discourse. The chapter further proposes (and illustrates) how imagistic and bicultural form of communication, plump with metaphor and image, can help to reframe the conversation of academic research, in both form and content.

Keywords Bicultural communication • Cixous • Grapholect • l'écriture feminine • Masculine discourse

In the previous chapter I discussed that being denied voice, or the expression of one's own ideas, experience and values, is a form of oppression. Yet the oppression of voicelessness is interesting as the oppressor isn't always aware of how he/she/we might be contributing anOther's lack of voice. In this chapter, I therefore explore the ways in which we might unwittingly maintain Others' voicelessness when we represent and speak of or

© The Author(s) 2018
G. Crimmins, *Theatricalising Narrative Research on Women Casual Academics*, Palgrave Studies in Gender and Education, https://doi.org/10.1007/978-3-319-71562-9_2

13

for them, and consider how we might instead speak *with* Others so that their stories can be both known and used to disrupt the structures that have prevented their voice being heard before. For, in addition to the lack of nuanced representations of and stories by women academics within the discourses of casualisation, the form of communication used within the discourse also contributes to their silencing. The reasons for this are multifaceted and intertwined, so in this chapter I reflect on the alienating force of traditional discourse; the problem of speaking for or of Others; and how Others – including women causal academics – need to find a language through which to express their/our understanding of the world so it can be heard, and used to create other ways of being in academia. I present these ideas as they informed my decision to employ the arts in re-presenting the lived experience of women casual academics (discussed in detail in Chap. 3), and are important ideas to ponder if you wish to engage in ethical research and communication. Therefore, this chapter rests on the idea that 'every seed destroys its container, or else there would be no fruition' (Scott-Maxwell 1979, 65).

WHEN FORM SUPPORTS SILENCING

In addition to the sex/gender/body-less-ness representation of casual academics presented as numbers in tables or shades of colour in bar graphs, the dominant academic discourse around casualisation employs third-person, 'hands-off', objective language and technical 'academic' terms. Yet such forms of rhetoric are said to create hierarchy and division between

the researcher,
the subject of the research,
and the audience
and further objectify the subject/s of the data (Blair et al. 1994; Hawkins 1989; Sefcovic and Bifano 2004).

In particular, most people who are the 'subject' of academic study or who might be interested in or benefit from a particular study are not academic and do not share the codes of communication predominantly used in research dissemination. Such codes are specialised, technical, terse, and so estrange people from the research to which they have contributed – if only in the form of taxes paid to fund the research. This is ethically problematic for me and I share Patricia Leavy's position when she claims that most academic research is totally inaccessible [as it is] loaded with jargon and prohibitive language. So, people don't want to read this stuff, nor can they. As a result, the average peer-reviewed article has an audience of 3–8 readers...That's astounding. when you consider the human and other resources put into research. (Carrigan 2017, 1)

Additionally, Hawkins (1989) recognised that the form of impersonal, 'neutral' scholarship both, perhaps ironically, renders the researcher invisible *and* positions him/her as the authority *on* the research 'subject'. Thus, in the current discourses around casualisation the scholar presenting objective 'facts' and figures about the casual academic is positioned not as an individual subjective being but as the expert (the knower) on the subject *of* the casual academic her/himself – and the causal academic is simultaneously silenced and positioned as the un-knower.

Relatedly, Bizzell (1992) uses the term 'grapholect' to describe the use of third person 'objective' language which suggests that the researcher is neutral in the research. Grapholect is particularly described as precise, concise, formal language, employed in a highly structured form of argument. Whilst recognising grapholect as a derivation of upper-class code of communication of the sixteenth, seventeenth and eighteenth centuries, Bizzell claims it is used to 'standardise' and 'normalise' a highly conservative and elitist communication style (1992). She also considers that the valued position of grapholect in academic journals suggests that only reason, separate from emotion, can produce 'proper' knowledge (Bizzell 1999). Finally, describing the persona of grapholect as 'male, and white, and economically privileged' (1999, 11) Bizzell describes how it propagates a conservative, elitist or even masculine form of knowing and communicating, which simultaneously discredits or silences the vernacular and feminine cognition and expression.

> I've left a space to pause here
>   as Bizzell's ideas are dense
>   and prompt a moment of reflection (and play)
> Grapholect – the pin striped, three-piece suit, monocle wearing Lord
> With a stiff upper lip and a plumb in his mouth
> mansplains
> to the pyjama-wearing casual academic, struggling to mark at 2am,
> all about her life

I consciously transgress 'the rules' of traditional academic discourse here (I've dropped my grapholect), because as Davies (2005) notes,

'You cannot tell a joke in this language, or write a poem, or sing a song. It is a language without human provenance or possibility' (Davies 2005, 1). Yet I do deliberately change out of my Sunday best (so to speak) in order to expose the restrictions and constructedness of 'academicspaek'.

But on a more serious note Bizzell's observations prompt to consider how I might avoid sm/Othering the stories of women casual academics in objective, all-knowing, unemotional, upper-class and inaccessible language.

Indeed, Bizzell's arguments are resonant with Spivak's (1988) discussion on the problem of using white, privileged, masculine forms of communication when presenting research on or 'about' Others. She specifically suggests that it is ethically irresponsible to investigate people/s from a different cultural base using the *so-claimed* universal concepts, frameworks and languages adopted by white western researchers. In her seminal text, *Can the Subaltern Speak?* Spivak (1988) argues that western academic thinking is produced in order to support western interests, and that research is consistently and fundamentally colonial, defining the 'other', the 'over there' subject, the object of study, as something from which knowledge should be extracted and brought back 'here' (Spivak 1988). She also claims that speaking *for* the disenfranchised can paradoxically silence them because a subaltern female's knowledge and means of communication become incomprehensible when translated into the masculine form of traditional discourse. That is, when the subaltern woman's story is contained within white middle-class masculine discourse, heavy with white Western middle-class ideology, the subaltern woman's story becomes mutated and her voice muted. So even when if she is invited to speak her truth she is not able to be heard.

We smother and Other when we lay our texts/words over the voice/s of research participants because the form/s of language we use are pregnant with philosophical, political and ideological implication, and our own positioning. Although this notion that communication inhabits a philosophical and ideological position may sound a little complex, I simply suggest that writing is never neutral. When we write we claim a relationship to knowledge and imply whether we think it is static (ahistorical and a-cultural) or if it is situated, constructed by the knower and informed by experience. Communication also establishes a particular type of relationship with the reader. For when we write 'we' or 'I' (instead of one), we make manifest that it is simply our personal perspective/s in relation to the idea/s that is being shared, not some universal truth; when we ask questions we welcome a conversation, we invite the reader to consider her or his own position on the matter, and we don't present ourselves as an all-knowing authority; when we share our personal stories/perspectives we acknowledge the existence of a multiplicity of stories/perspectives, none greater or lesser than our own; and when we break up a theoretical discussion with 'pause points' or explanation we invite reflection, not necessarily assimilation. In these ways, and many more, our communication inhabits a philosophical and political position with the ideas presented and a relationship with the audience of the communication.

Correspondingly, although Spivak's (1988) specific polemic argues against the western re-presentation of *the subaltern* woman, her argument appears relevant to other contexts, cultures and peoples, including women casual academics. In advancing the idea that a subaltern female cannot be heard or understood using traditional academic lenses and discourse, Spivak illuminates the notion that the subaltern woman's truth is intertwined with, and made intelligible through her aesthetic form/s of communication. This idea compels to consider if other marginalised peoples have a specific aesthetic through which they understand and communicate their experience. And when Spivak states that unless western intellectuals take into account subaltern women's aesthetic way of knowing and communicating they will continue to speak on behalf *of* and so silence subaltern women, she invites me to consider if we/women casual academics also have a distinct way of knowing that is intertwined with a particular form of communication. And if so, how might I recognise and re-present it? I therefore engage with ideas around how women might prefer to communicate, and if a feminine way of communicating might more congruently communicate our lived experience than a masculine form of grapholect.

A FEMININE WAY OF KNOWING

By way of contextualisation I feel it is important to draw a distinction between the notion of a woman's way of knowing and feminine ways of knowing. My position, which I share with Belenky et al. (1986), Gilligan (2008), and Simson (2005) is that women's and men's thinking do not fall neatly into two distinct epistemological camps, never the twain to meet. The claim that men and women have exclusive ways of knowing and communicating is essentialist and has been used to justify gender inequality for centuries. Yet I do acknowledge that due to the influence of cultural gender conditioning (Harding 1988; MacKinnon 2006), women and men have a *tendency* to think in ways that are often distinctive from one another (Gilligan 2008; Simson 2005), though not exclusive to one sex or another.

For instance, Carol Gilligan (1982) suggests that feminine logic incorporates a concern with care, relationships, and context, within their judgement-making process. In doing so she accepts that women have a propensity to think differently from men but denies that the difference is inferior to male reasoning, or that it should preclude them from being able to engage in intellectual work (Simson 2005). Similarly, Belenky et al. (1986) and Halpern (2012) consider the central roles of care, connection and relationships within female cognition and propose that women are less inclined than men to engage in 'separate knowing' or detached and impartial judgement. Moreover, these positions are supported by Lips (2010) who uses neurobiological studies to demonstrate that male brains tend to divide cognitive tasks between hemispheres and so male thinking is likely to be localised and compartmentalised. She also finds that women's brains tend to operate more malleably or holistically and process tasks between the hemispheres more frequently. Lips' (2010) study thus suggests that women's brains reveal a *tendency* towards interconnectedness and support the notion of a distinctly feminine way of knowing.

Extending this notion (of a feminine way of knowing) further, Simson (2005) posits that publicly re-presenting feminine ways of knowing is important as it draws attention to significant and worthy contributions that women make to human reasoning and knowledge. Similarly, Mills (1988) explains that an advantage of acknowledging a feminine perspective, and considering the world from the stance of other disadvantaged groups more generally, is the ability to recognise the limitations of a detached and disinterested perspective. He further claims that feminine ways of knowing also recognise the impact of emotion and affect in developing understanding, which again exposes the myth of an objective, universal, ahistorical, notion of truth and knowledge.

These ideas persuaded me to consider what form/s of communication I might use to unearth and re-present the lived experience and understanding of Others. As I was particularly interested in the lived experience of women casual academics – people who identify as women and who share a professional status but live in different countries, identify with different races and religions, have different colours of skin, experience diverse socio-economic statuses, and have different sexual orientations and dis/abilities – I simply sought to understand how women generally might express the experience of their lives.

I looked to the work of Hélène Cixous for insight as she is considered one of the most influential theorists around feminine and feminist communication. Cixous' (1976) fundamental position is that women each have a story to tell, and that our stories are most clearly communicated through "l'écriture feminine" or women's writing. Cixous reflects that throughout history women have been defined and restricted by both a masculine gaze *and* discourse, but we can choose to either perpetuate the passive female role, by continuing to employ masculine communication structures, or we can adopt strategies of resistance. Resistance, for Cixous, requires subverting both the masculine concept *and* language structure, as she too recognised that all forms of communication inhabit a philosophical and political position (1976).

A FEMININE WAY OF COMMUNICATING

Cixous (1976) identified that the characteristics of l'écriture feminine include the sweeping away of syntax, and abandoning the linearity and orderly structure of masculine/traditional communication, and through using a fusion of poetry, philosophy and feminist polemic Cixous simultaneously explained and practiced l'écriture feminine. In so doing Cixous creates a cohesion between form and content. Later, in 1998, Cixous, with Clément (1986) discussed how image and drawing can also be used within l'écriture feminine, and stressed the importance of the improvisational and iterative processes of communicating. She suggested that women ought to sketch, play with images, and improvise by using free-association in order to reject the teleological structures of masculine writing and resist the notion of the perfect and complete sentence or argument.

Cixous' ideas give me licence to be fully present and interested in the ideas with which I engage, they allow me to be me *in* my writing, and to worry less about *how* I write so that I can concentrate on *what* I write. The ideas allow me to do away with the post write edit/cleanse so that I can concentrate on the new idea that the previous has spawned. As a result of engaging with Cixous' ideas, the substance of my communication, perhaps ironically, takes priority over its form (even though I am encouraged to play with the form).

rigid lines
of cause and effect
with
stance/premise/evidence/citation to support/full stop/upper case letter
recurring
constrains my energy
and dulls my argument

But Cixous'
freeing of form
reflect and en/gender a-feminine-way-of-knowing-and-telling
thrill and energise
unzip restraints
and allow ideas to free fall form

Cixous' theories have also influenced many Other women, and spurred much experimentation and theorising. For instance, Chen (2011) expanded the characteristics of l'écriture feminine to include a concern with the social role of women, to focus on the experiences of women, and a preference for emotional and imaginative insight, intuition and synaesthesia. Billingham (2010) incorporated the stylistic features of imagistic collage, wordplay and intertextuality as characteristics of l'écriture feminine, and reflected that when literary codes are broken so too are old habits of thought.

Pause.

For Billingham (2010), when literary codes are broken so too are old habits of thought. This can also be understood to mean that new forms of communication create opportunities for new meanings to emerge.

FORM SEEDS THE CONDITIONS FOR NEW IDEAS

This reflection on the role of form in seeding or creating the conditions for new ideas and processes of thinking to occur invites me to consider more fully the inter-relationship between form and content, and to recognise that just as new forms can create the circumstance for new ideas and stories to emerge, so new ideas need new forms to embody and reflect them. It calls for new bottles for new wine.

This idea (of finding new forms to embody new ideas) is reflected in the work and ideas of Laurel Richardson, an American sociologist known for her work in qualitative sociology and the sociology of gender. When Richardson (1997) chose to explore the feminine experience of academia, she felt the need to 'de-discipline' her academic communication by breaking with the conventions of masculinely structured discourse, including the suppression of her own voice. She rejected what she considered to be the duplicity of adopting a supposedly objective voice/stance, when for her *the researcher is ever-present in the text*, no matter how it might be otherwise perceived or disguised. Richardson therefore experimented with drama, narrative poetry, lyrical poetry, prose poems, comedy and autobiography in her scholarship in order to both reject and hold up for scrutiny science's 'omniscient voice from nowhere' (Richardson 1997, 5).

In addition, Cixous' recommendations for sketching and using image in communicating and forming ideas resonate with the ideas presented by philosopher Susanne Langer in 1942 and 1962. Langer suggested that images precede linguistic codes of communication, that we first come to know and understand through visualising images and scenarios, and that we subsequently interpret and communicate our understanding in words. Hence, for Langer, imagistic narrative both precede and supersede a linguistic code of knowing (1942). Langer also believed that narrative image is closer to emotionally lived experience than linguistically coded narrative, and that intramental imagistic narratives were in fact the 'catalyst' that initiated the evolution of speech (1962, 41–42). That is, through a need to communicate one's narrative knowing/images wo/man transferred images into the linguistic signs of communication. Thus, for Langer, a primordial practice of imagistic and narrative knowing played a central role in the evolution of speech communication.

These ideas are rich, so rich. And they are conceptualised by women philosophers, artists, and scholars. Women who are so often invisible in the history of philosophy and ideas. As a feminist, I thus deliberately and proudly lean into the ideas by wise women of before and since, to engage in my research. The ideas presented by Cixous, Richardson and Langer perhaps disrupt your previously held beliefs about how we know and communicate. They might subvert what we have understood about the neutrality of and primacy of words in the genealogy of knowledge construction and communication.

You may wish to sit with these ideas for a while, to give yourself time to pause, perhaps to readjust your thinking as Cixous, Richardson and

Langer's ideas have the potential to open up rich possibility for *how* we re-present our research; they might grant licence to draw, photograph, sculpt, film, photograph, create theatre, and communicate of yourself, as image is the primary signifier in our understanding.

BICULTURAL COMMUNICATION

Yet, as you're reading this you'll note that I'm not solely, or even predominantly, presenting my ideas in image, or Cixous' notion of free association. Though may have noticed the odd metaphor, plenty of the first person, the occasional section of text set out differently from the rest, and maybe a poem. This is because whilst I'm fully enthused by, and even feel liberated by, the qualities of l'écriture feminine, and of the primal relationship between image, knowledge and communicating, I use (for the most part) full sentence structures and plenty of in-text citations, my grammar is generally correct, as are my spelling/s because I would like to share the ideas within this book. I want them to inform your practice (and maybe the practice of others who engage with your work). And one of the main ways to support this aim is through publication/s. When ideas are published, printed, copied and pasted to friends via emails, tweeted, re-tweeted and blogged, when they are made known across continent and cultures they can be engaged with, adopted, critiqued, and can extend existing ideas and discourses. But without publication, it is more difficult for ideas to penetrate (y/our) practice. Ideas need to be known to have any impact, and discourse that is recognisable in either form *or* content is more likely to be published.

For instance, Bach et al. (1996) identify that those who fail to acknowledge, and to a certain extent *follow* the rules of discourse are often assigned to the ranks of marginality, outside the mainstream, 'dismissed as square pegs or cranks, or even invited to leave the community altogether' (1996, 413). Indeed, they note that most feminine and feminist scholarship remains unpublished and fails to find a home within the academic discourses it seeks to dialogue with, extend, or even contest. In addition, without the platform of scholarship and its audience, we (feminist researchers), become further unvoiced. In particular, Fleckenstein (1996) warned women academics against completely rejecting scholarship as a mode of communication, as if we rely on images and feminine codes alone 'women just exchange one kind of silence for another' (1996, 924).

These ideas created a dilemma. I questioned whether to create an authentic body of work in a radically new form, with the high likelihood that it would fail to penetrate the main academic discourses I wish to contest, or to adopt traditional structures and slowly but meaningly adapt and amend the structures to suit my purpose. The latter approach I found opens up opportunities for creative adaptation, and the merging of some conventions of masculine scholarship with new forms or content. It offers possibilities for a broadening of what is considered publishable and therefore deemed 'knowable' in academia. Sefcovic and Bifano (2004) call such a form of scholarship a 'hybrid' form, and suggest that new and potentially radical content situated within masculine forms of scholarship can derive an authority through referencing impeccable sources and structuring arguments logically using traditional essay structures. Or, alternatively, that juxtaposing passages of first person narrative, reflection and illustration within traditional argumentative structures can create possibilities for academic acceptance and subversion (Sefcovic and Bifano 2004). These playful devices achieve mainstream credibility for new and potentially radical scholarship.

I therefore, 'play' with form and structure in this book. I use traditional, recognisable structures, alongside passages of personal reflection, word play and the odd image, and by doing so employ a hybrid form of scholarship that Blankenship and Robson (1995) call bicultural communication. I also attempt to follow a communication pattern described by Susanne Gannon as zig-zagging 'between categories, that produce knowledge in the gaps between analysis and creativity, reason and emotion, intellectual and aesthetic, mind and body, academic and everyday' (Gannon 2005, 629), as I established earlier, that new forms create possibilities for new content and ideas.

CLOSING CONSIDERATIONS

Therefore, in this chapter I show why and how it is possible to stretch the (p)restrictive confines of masculine communication by consciously adopting and adapting a feminine way of knowing and communicating with masculine discursive forms, to create a bicultural form of communication. I also offer the provocation that Image pre-existed the use of words and that images in our mind's eye prompted the development and evolution of a verbal and written language. Yet, I suggest also that we ought to not completely reject traditional discourse as such a move could further silence women within language and text-dominant cultures. Instead I both endorse and use bicultural communication which embraces some features of traditional written expression playfully merged with imagistic, reflective, and expressive forms of communication. In particular, I use elements of traditional discourse (such as honouring sources of insight and influence through the use of academic citation) alongside 'feminine' forms of communication (self-reflection, poetry, and a general loosening of discursive conventions). I use the 'I' word, and allow full sentence structures to tango with rhetorical questions; fragments of sentence to waltz with run-ons; topic sentences to foxtrot with images, and some sentences begin with and'. And I do so to engage an audience in the lived experience of women casual academics in a form which embraces and celebrates women's way/s of knowing and communicating.

REFERENCES

Bach, T. E., Blair, C., Nothstine, W. L., & Pym, A. L. (1996). How to Read "How to Get Published". *Communication Quarterly, 44*(4), 399–422. http://www.tandfonline.com/toc/rcqu20/current#.VB-Za5Ta7uA

Belenky, M. F., Clinchy, B. M., Goldberger, N. R., & Tarule, J. M. (1986). *Women's Ways of Knowing: The Development of Self, Voice and Mind*. New York: Basic Books.

Billingham, S. (2010). Ecriture Au Trans-Féminine: Trish Salah's Wanting in Arabic. *Canadian Literature, 205*, 33–51. https://canlit.ca/article/ecriture-au-trans-feminine

Bizzell, P. (1992). *Academic Discourse and Critical Consciousness (in English)*. Pittsburgh: University of Pittsburgh Press.

Bizzell, P. (1999). Hybrid Academic Discourses: What, Why, How. *Composition Studies, 27*(2), 7–21. http://www.uc.edu/journals/composition-studies.html

Blair, C., Brown, J. R., & Baxter, L. A. (1994). Disciplining the Feminine. *Quarterly Journal of Speech, 80*(4), 383–409. https://doi.org/10.1080/00335639409384084

Blankenship, J., & Robson, D. (1995). A 'feminine' style in women's political discourse: An exploratory essay. *Communication Quarterly, 43*(3), 353–366. https://doi.org/10.1080/01463379509369982

Carrigan, M. (2017, May 8). An Interview with Patricia Leavy About Research Design in Contemporary Times. *The Sociological Imagination*. http://sociologicalimagination.org/archives/19315

Chen, R. (2011). Highlighting Women's Life – Analysis of Distinguishing Feature of Contemporary Feminine Prose. *Asian Social Science, 7*(3), 145–149. https://doi.org/10.5539/ass.v7n3p145

Cixous, H. (1976). The Laugh of the Medusa. *Signs, 1*(4), 875–893. http://www.jstor.org/stable/3173239

Cixous, H., & Clément, C. (1986). *The Newly Born Woman* (trans: Wing, B.). Minneapolis: University of Minnesota Press.

Davies, B. (2005). The (Im)Possibility of Intellectual Work in Neoliberal Regimes. *Discourse: Studies in the Cultural Politics of Education, 26*(1), 1–14. https://doi.org/10.1080/01596300500039310

Fleckenstein, K. S. (1996). Images, Words, and Narrative Epistemology. *College English, 58*(8), 914–933. http://www.jstor.org/stable/378229

Gannon, S. (2005). "The Tumbler": Writing an/Other in Fiction and Performance Ethnography. *Qualitative Inquiry, 11*(4), 622–627. https://doi.org/10.1177/1077800405276811

Gilligan, C. (1982). *In a different voice.* Cambridge, MA: Harvard University Press.

Gilligan, C. (2008). Moral Orientation and Moral Development. In A. Bailey & C. J. Cuomo (Eds.), *The Feminist Philosophy Reader* (pp. 467–477). Boston: McGraw-Hill.

Halpern, D. F. (2012). *Sex Differences in Cognitive Abilities* (4th ed.). Hillside: Erlbaum.

Harding, S. (1988). *The Science Question in Feminism.* Ithaca: Cornell University Press.

Hawkins, K. (1989). Exposing Masculine Science: An Alternative Feminist Approach to the Study of Women's Communication. In K. Carter & C. Spitzack (Eds.), *Doing Research on Women's Communication: Perspectives on Theory and Method* (pp. 40–64). Norwood: Ablex.

Langer, S. K. (1942). *Philosophy in a New Key.* Cambridge: Harvard University Press.

Langer, S. K. (1962). *Philosophical Sketches.* Baltimore: Johns Hopkins University Press.

Lips, H. M. (2010). *A New Psychology of Women: Gender, Culture and Ethnicity.* Mountain View: Mayfield Publishing.

MacKinnon, C. (2006). Difference and Domination: On Sex Discrimination. In E. Hackett & S. Haslanger (Eds.), *Theorising Feminisms: A Reader.* New York: Oxford University Press.

Mills, C. W. (1988). Alternative Epistemologies. In L. M. Alcoff (Ed.), *Epistemology: The Big Questions.* Maiden: Blackwell.

Richardson, L. (1997). Skirting a Pleated Text: De-disciplining an Academic Life. *Qualitative Inquiry, 3*(3), 295–303. https://doi.org/10.1177/107780049700300303

Scott-Maxwell, F. (1979). *The Measure of My Days* (1st ed.). New York: Penguin Books.

Sefcovic, E. M. I., & Bifamo, D. T. (2004). Creating a Rhetorical Home for Feminists in the "Master's House" of the Academy: Toward a Gendered

Taxonomy of Form and Content. *Women and Language, 27*(1), 53–62. https://www.highbeam.com/doc/1G1-121672314.html

Simson, R. S. (2005). Feminine Thinking. *Social Theory and Practice, 31*(1), 1–26. http://www.jstor.org/stable/23558685

Spivak, G. (1988). Can the Subaltern Speak? In P. Williams & L. Christman (Eds.), *Colonial Discourse and Postcolonial Theory: A Reader* (pp. 66–109). New York: Colombia University Press.

CHAPTER 3

Orienting My Map to North

Abstract This chapter shares the complexity and human dimension(ality) of arts-informed narrative research. It considers the need for alignment between a research methodology, methods, and communication, yet illustrates how research doesn't always journey along a pre-planned path. In sharing my embodied resistance to a planned narrative analysis, I reflect on the need for regular, fully embodied reflexivity to fulfil the overall aims of a research project. Further, the chapter explores the congruence between narrative, Arts-based and feminist approaches to research, and shares an innovative narrative restorying practice which merges Gee's (An introduction to discourse analysis: theory and method, 2nd edn. Routledge, London, 2005) process of data gathering with a new materialist approach to capturing data that 'glows' (MacLure, Crit Methodol 13(4):228–232, 2013). In so doing, new and promiscuous research processes are celebrated.

Keywords Narrative analysis • Narrative restorying • Affective intensities • Feminist research

Being gifted a story, invites a re-gifting

Seeing that
the fully lived experience of women casual academics is yet to be voiced
(Arnot and Reay 2007);

© The Author(s) 2018   27
G. Crimmins, *Theatricalising Narrative Research on Women Casual Academics*, Palgrave Studies in Gender and Education,
https://doi.org/10.1007/978-3-319-71562-9_3

straightjacketed by the boxes into which she is invited to commit her age,
highest qualification, length of 'service'... classifications deemed worthy of
'knowing';
drowned by the acadmicspeak of the researcher/the expert on casualisa-
tion/the authority *on* the casual academic.
I seek out their yet to be storied stories in the voice/s of the storyteller

Yet when stories are gifted, we must receive and respond, not know them,
or think we know them, before the story is shared;
and once offered we ought not to slice and dice into manageable and analys-
able bite-size pieces
the experience stories hold within
Instead, we must hold them whole, and contemplate ways to re-gift them so
that others can know and feel them wholly

Committed to unearthing the experience of women casual academics
and to elevate their voice/s above the din of statistics (of gender disadvantage and the rises in casualisation of academia) I sought to find a way to
both gather stories and communicate them in a way that bears witness to
them and makes them available for others to see and hear.

In this chapter, I therefore explicitly share the particularity, complexity,
and human-ness of arts-informed research by showing how I orientated
my compass to north (to making manifest the lived experience of casual
academics) in order to create alignment between a research methodology,
research methods, and how I chose to communicate the research. I also
reveal that research does not always journey along a pre-planned path, but
requires researcher reflexivity, pit stops and re-planning, so that the overall
aims of the research are met.

As I suggested in Chap. 1 I accept, along with Hardy (1968) and
Bruner (1986) that we come to know and communicate what we hold to
be true through narratives. The world is storied and we understand the
world and our role within it in stories. Narratives, and the narrative images
we construct and deconstruct have birthed languages and inter-personal
communication (Langer 1942, 1962). In alignment with these I chose to
uncover the experience of women casual academics using narrative inquiry.

Narrative inquiry is a research methodology that's based on the idea
that 'the way humans experience the world through the stories they tell'
(Connelly and Clandinin 1990, 1). It is also said to have the capacity to
preserve the integrity (including the messiness, richness and texture) of
each story by using the storytellers' actual words to capture and re-present

their lived experience (Etherington 2004). Finally, and – in alignment with Deleuze's argument that we express ourselves through images and sensations which inhabit an inherent 'logic of sense', as opposed to logic of reason (1990) – stories unearthed through a narrative inquiry often follow their own internal logic and rhythm. That is, stories regularly conflate the linearity and teleology of causal logic and reason.

Stories can thus m

           e   e   r
                a   n   d

pause,
repeat and off-shoot.

NARRATIVE AND FEMINIST RESEARCH

Another central feature of narrative inquiry I'm drawn to as a feminist researcher is its capacity to provide opportunities of voice for women and other marginalised groups. For instance, Davis and Skilton-Sylvester recognise the emancipatory role of narrative inquiry which they describe as a medium for those '"at the bottom" to speak alongside their more recognized, and published, colleagues' (Davis and Skilton-Sylvester 2004, 389). Bell (2002) similarly suggests that it functions democratically by offering 'opportunity for marginalized groups to participate in knowledge construction in the academy' (2002, 209) and Boje (1995) considers that the presentation of stories from marginalised groups within large organisations can be creatively liberating as they expose and celebrate a multiplicity of stories and storytellers. Moreover, narrative inquiry is often designed to 'touch base with the variety of real life stories women provide about themselves' (Lugones et al. 1983, 21). Thus, for all these reasons I chose a narrative inquiry to uncover the lived experience of women casual academics.

I also found a narrative epistemology and feminist lens to create a cohesive conceptual framework through which to study and present the lives of women casual academics. Feminism is concerned with the condition of women within society and their relationship to power, whilst feminist research is committed to changing the subordinate status of females in society by making manifest the lives and experience of women (Hesse-Biber et al. 2004). In particular, Nissen (2011) contends that feminist research encourages the marginalised to discuss their/our lived experiences; and explicitly addresses the issue of finding a voice (Nissen 2011). A further distinguishing factor in feminist research is its acceptance of the pre-rational and extra-rational knowing of women (Merriam et al. 2007). It neither ignores nor essentialises women's multiple ways of knowing (Belenky et al. 1986) which are said to include intuition (Merriam et al. 2007), a feminine ethic (Gilligan 1982), imagistic knowing (Fleckenstein 1996), and connected and context-rich knowing (Belenky et al. 1986; Gilligan 1982). Indeed, within feminist research the female experience in its entirety becomes an arena of interest, investigation and dissemination. Finally, one of the main objectives of feminist research is to recognise and challenge the androcentrally bias within science and research (Harding 1987) by situating women as subject and object/participant in research, and signalling an important expansion in what is considered researchable and what are considered legitimate research processes (Hesse-Biber et al. 2004). I therefore conceive a clear congruence between a narrative and feminist conceptual framework.

ARTS-INFORMED NARRATIVE RESEARCH

Yet, a feminist and narrative melded research methodology will not protect the stories shared within a narrative inquiry from being trapped in/to traditional discourse, sm/Othered of their original lilt or meaning. Mindful that the casual academic's voice can be drowned-out or mutated by the acadmicspeak of the researcher/the expert on casualisation/the authority on the casual academic, I chose to reject traditional masculine discourses and consider the arts, and theatre more specifically, as valuable in re-presenting women casual academics' stories in a form that is congruent with their content, and so a suitable form through which their experience can be made known. Indeed, Barone and Eisner (1997) reflect that narratives possess the presence of expressive, contextualised, and vernacular forms of language that reflect that of the original storyteller.

In addition, the inherent narrativity of experience and aesthetic quality of stories are congruent with artistic representation. As Sikes and Gale contemplate, stories have the ability to stimulate us aesthetically, to 'open our senses' (Sikes and Gale 2006, chap. 2), and Richardson (2000), suggests that stories transfer easily to creative representation and possess the capacity to re-create and not merely show lived experience. This notion that artistic forms can both reflect and evoke fully embodied experience was first identified by Dewey in 1934 when he claimed that art does something different from leading to an experience – it constitutes one (Dewey 1934). Such evocation and re-experience, I feel, can sensitise us to one another and support our empathetic listening to and with one another.

I chose therefore to re-present the stories of women casual academics in an artistic form of communication, and so the methodology I employed coupled narrative inquiry with arts-informed research. Arts-informed research is a form of qualitative research in the social sciences that is informed by but not based in the arts. Its main aim is to enhance our understanding of the human condition through alternative (to conventional) representational forms of inquiry (Cole and Knowles 2008) and in practice, it merges the methodical and rigorous processes of social science inquiry with the artistic and imaginative form and qualities of the arts (Cole and Knowles 2008). Arts-informed inquiry is also used to reach audiences, emotionally and cognitively, within and beyond the academy (Sikes and Gale 2006, chap. 2).

Whilst there is no one accepted definition of, or approach to, arts-informed inquiry (Diamond and Mullen 1999) it does tend to include:

- the use of expressive and vernacular language;
- the promotion of empathy or engagement with the audience;
- the presence of an aesthetic form or forms in data collection and/or analysis and/or representation;
- integrity in the relationship between the research topic and its form;
- the opportunity to explore multiple perspectives; and
- reflexivity and the personal signature or presence of the researcher. (Adapted from Barone and Eisner 1997, 73–78 and Knowles and Cole 2008, 61–62; cited in Ewing and Hughes 2008, 514).

I found alignment between some of these conventions and my wish to provide opportunity of voice to marginalised women. First, as I discussed in Chap. 2, many women have a tendency towards a particular/feminine way of knowing and communicating, so there seems to be integrity in form of communication that uses the actual words and expression of participants. Further, arts-informed research incorporates a concern for emotion and empathy which is also compatible with a feminist preoccupation with extra-rational knowing of lived experience. Also, arts-informed research goes beyond creating an objective description or analysis of experience, to conveying or stimulating it. As Alexander (2003, 3) claims, 'artists not only describe what they experience; they create virtual experiences in language, space, time or sound so that others can grasp what they perceive directly, through encountering a new work of art' (cited in Ewing and Hughes 2008, 514). So, I felt arts-informed processes could help create congruence between narrative content and form, and possess the capacity to embrace and centralise women's ways of communicating their experience.

More specifically, I decided to employ theatre as the form through which to re-present the stories of women casual academics as drama can accommodate the *process* of living, which is experienced and understood tangentially, chronologically (through time) but not linearly (Deleuze 1990). Theatre, as is life, is also fully embodied (Merleau-Ponty 1962) and dynamic. It is thus able to re-present fully embodied experience, replete with a capability to express the physical, emotional and psychological experience of individuals.

I therefore, determined to employ a narrative inquiry to uncover the stories of experience by women casual academics, followed by a narrative analysis of the stories to identify the central themes to be re-presented in the form of a drama. I had it all

> straight – in my head. I was ready…. But,
> as with living,
> research practice often deviates from 'the plan'.

A Diversion to Keep Me on My Path

The initial research process followed this recipe as laid out in my research proposal. I invited six women casual academics from across three universities in Australia to share with me the stories of their experience, through narrative (unstructured) interviews. I used narrative interviewing as it's designed to expand the restrictions and inherent bias of structured and formal interviews and seeks to disrupt the hierarchical relationship between interviewer and 'interviewee often established in traditional interviewing processes' (Gubrium and Holstein 2002). Through undertaking narrative interviews, I sought to 'cede control' of both the interview scene to the interviewee, and assumed the role of active listener (Jones 2004) to give authority to the storyteller, whom I acknowledged 'as the one who knows and tells' (Kramp 2004, 111). In so doing I listened care-fully to the yet to be voiced (Arnot and Reay 2007) stories of women casual academics.

The interviews, and subsequent email and phone conversations uncovered layer upon layer of lives lost, lived, and living in academia. The women participants shared stories of emotional experience (Richards 2011), alongside critique of the inequitable and de-humanising structures of contemporary academia; and they accepted responsibility and demonstrated agency in their work, yet expressed a lack of control and power. Twelve months of stories and meaning were generously shared and relationships were formed.

Yet, holding the women's rich and personal tapestry of lived experience in my hands felt like both a significant honour *and* responsibility, and I began to experience a strong resistance to using a narrative analysis (to determine the main themes and ideas in their stories). I feared that the process of dissecting the women's stories into themes for analysis might distort their narrative flow and disrupt the women's voice within the story; it might limit the possibility of establishing the context of each described event or character description, and diminish the idiosyncratic nature of their individualised experience. I shared Richards' apprehension when she reflected that she might 'trespass with muddy feet into the hearts of her participants' were she to deconstruct the lived experience/stories of participants into un/usable categories of data (Richards 2011, 11).

I responded to my resistance by pausing and just sitting with the stories for a while –

for a
   l
   o
   n
   g
   while,
seemingly doing nothing.

Yet all the time, in my seeming stasis, I was thinking (and feeling) about how I might validate and share the women's stories without dissecting and scrutinising them as if they were discreet cells of data. And even though I knew this pause in research 'productivity' wasn't written into my 'projected timeline' I *felt* a physiological and well as psychological opposition to analysing the women's stories (though could not determine which was stronger – or whether it indeed mattered). My 'feeling of body' was indeed a reflection of my cognition, and my cognitive resistance narrative represented my embodied feeling of resistance (Gallese and Wojciehowski 2011). So, my whole being responded with pause, and I simply accepted that it was less harmful to do nothing, for a while, than to potentially undermine the integrity of the women's stories so generously shared. I believe that

We cannot slice, dice and trim the narrative to know the knower
as the fleshy story reveals the whole

It is in its detail, the before and after that its entirety lies
We need to hear her whole, for her-story is important

The experience also taught me of the need to regularly check the alignment of all research processes against the overall aims of a project, and that what we *feel* as researchers, is important. Indeed, being open to how we feel *and* think about the research processes with which we engage helps us to maintain both our integrity *and* that of the project. Unexpected internal resistances can keep us on our toes, they're indexes that something is out of alignment (Pagis 2009), and remind us to keep checking our research compass to (re)orient to north (to the main aims of the research project) so that we can find a way around unexpected obstacles.

So, as a result of the pause – and supported by Gould's (1996) and Etherington's (2004) understanding that human life and agency cannot be 'explained', and Hendry's (2010) reflection that experience, understood narratively, requires 'interpretation' (not explanation) and a communication distinct from written argument – I readjusted my plan to *restory* the women's narratives, instead of employing a narrative analysis. The restoryed narrative would be performed as a theatre piece. In this particular project, pointing my compass due North required privileging and individualising of women casual academics' experience and honouring the integrity of their stories.

RESTORYING THE DATA

As a feminist researcher, I consciously refused to engage in a traditional/ masculine narrative analysis process of coding data, I chose instead to undertake a data/narrative restorying process, and in doing so, to embrace 'other ways' of doing and knowing in academia. I therefore illustrate below how I developed a new approach to narrative restorying, in a bid to re-present the lived experience of women casual academics. The approach I used merged what is understood as a holistic restorying process developed by Gee in 2005, with an embodied and affective approach of selecting narratives to restory inspired by Ringrose and Renold's (2014) notion of affective intensities, and MacLure's (2013) proposition that data can glow with/in us. I thus discuss how I weaved together Gee's (2005) processes with Ringrose and Renold's (2014) and MacLure's (2013) musings, into a data restorying processes not yet fully 'named/famed' as a recognised research process. Indeed, as much of feminist research is considered to be outside-in the academy we (as feminist researchers) get to 'create and play with promiscuous feminist methodologies… [which] are always in-the-making and already ahead of what we think they are' (Childers et al. 2013, 507).

The outside-in-the-academy
below stairs
status of feminist research/er
affords us the opportunity of scholarly promiscuity;
borrowing,
blurring,
merging,
bower-bird-ing
creating new, not-done-before, not yet 'proven'
or male named
methods and processes.
We make the most of our outside-ness to do and be other'wise' women-academics

Correspondingly, much of feminist research is thought to be a messy practice of inquiry that transgresses imposed boundaries or assumptions about what counts as research, and defies easy classification (Lather 2006). Consequently, I do not have a label or cohesive title to apply to the approach to restorying with which I engaged (in the process of transforming women's stories into verbatim drama). Instead of labelling, naming and owning it, I will try instead to simply describe the promiscuous, in-the-making method (Childers et al. 2013) of 'handling the data' I employed.

In an aim to preserve both the words and intended meaning of the words within the stories shared by women casual academics, I initially employed Gee's (2005) holistic method of grouping data into units of narrative. This process allowed me to keep large sections or chunks of the participant's stories together, as story units in order to maintain the integrity of the situated and contextualised meanings contained within told stories

(Lieblich 2006). It also enabled me to preserve the women's stories 'verbatim' and to place the meaning of the women's lived experience – contained in the words, phrases and structures of their communication – at the centre of the research re-presentation.

I next grouped what I understood to be the main ideas within the stories together by noticing a repetition of ideas or experiences within a number of narratives, and used them to form the basis of the main scenes in the drama:

Scene 1:   Why would you be a casual tutor?
Scene 2:   And then there's this long wait in between semesters
Scene 3:   But the biggest problem with casual work is financial
Scene 4:   Delta Dawn, what's that flower you have on?
Scene 5:   There's nothing you can do, you can't speak up
Epilogue: This is the complex part of being sessional...

Once I'd loosely identified the focus of each scene I began to order and reorder the narratives within the scenes so that a dialogue between the women's experiences could emerge. For instance, I noticed that several of the women's stories focused on time – the amount of time they spend on certain activities, the time they get up, the way they use time – and grouped these together as dialogue:

Sharon: week five's very intensive, that's a really intense time. And around week eight and nine that's when they all come in again. So, during the semester I work seven days a week always, like the entire semester there's never – I schedule myself so that I work early in the morning.

Sharon: So I will get up anywhere from 3:30 and then I will work for a few hours and then take a break for breakfast. So I have a good work schedule... it's almost like having two days in one.

Lyn: And I work weekends as well – Oh yeah, you have to. You don't ever take a day off during the semester

Yet at the end of the 'creating dialogue and action' process, I had gathered and placed over nine hours of narrative into six scenes, and knew that to create an accessible and engaging drama – 'to give listening ears to the voices that often go unheard' (Wake 2010, 3) – I would have to radically reduce the length of the drama. This deeply troubled me.

I respected Richards' (2011) conviction that participants' stories represent their truths, and Wake's (2013) suggestion that when a writer or dramatist omits someone's story from a play altogether it results in a sort of double silencing, where 'the silenced and traumatised are silenced and traumatised again… and the rhetoric of the social and political efficacy of verbatim theatre becomes empty' (Gibson 2011, 12).

This was a dilemma I felt strongly and through negotiation with the participants I began the process of editing the women participants' stories to create a research narrative with which people could engage fully.

Yet the editing stage of the project was the most time and heart-consuming task I undertook during this project

Pause.

Yes, cutting out
~~the sigh,~~
~~the explanation,~~
~~the repetition,~~
~~the aside,~~
~~the joke,~~
~~the non-sequitur,~~
~~the apology~~…
was the most time and heart-consuming task I undertook during this project.

I spent days/weeks/months reading and re-reading each scene several times, ensuring that that the storylines and extracts that appeared resonant to the women, because they seemed most significant or meaningful to each participant were retained in the script, were retained in the drama, whilst other sections were lost. Significance was indicated by a heightened emotion in the telling (shown through a change in volume, use of pause, lack of/animated gesture, lack of/eye contact, etc.). I also ensured that a significant 'amount' of story shared by each participant featured in the drama so that each woman's story could be known. But painfully, and through negotiation with the women participants, I merged some stories/dialogue and omitted sections of storyline. So, line by line and little by little the repeated and most emotionally significant moments of stories, and moments of narrative from each participant, were retained and reordered, and created the basis for a drama script.

Yet, as I've already reflected, as a feminist researcher I do not ascribe to thematic analysis and did not want to simply re-present stories as themes discussed repeatedly by many if not all participants. So, I responded to MacLure's (2013) invitation to engage with data in a way that is as a counterpart to the masculine logocentric approach to data interpretation, classification, and representation to preserve the integrity of the individual experience and the idiosyncratic phrases and reflections of the women participants. In particular, I developed a restorying process based on MacLure's (2013) understanding of the 'productive capacity for wonder that resides and radiates in data, or rather in the entangled relation of data-and-researcher' (MacLure 2013, 228), and her insight that our materiality intra-acts with the materiality of data to create in us a sense of wonder in us, and so 'wonder-full data. MacLure (2013) also muses that wonder resides in our bodies as well as our minds, so that when we engage in some data we may feel an affect in our gut or in the quickening of a heartbeat, and though we often recognise its impact we may not be able to describe why some data emotionally arrests us (and why some doesn't). Inspired by this new materialist conceptualisation, I re-read and re-listened (again) to the stories presented by the women casual academics – this time listening to my body and breath, identifying and collecting the moments of narrative that resonated with me most, that made me gasp or arrested my breath. I then simply gathered together the stories that g(r)asped me or created a kind of 'glow' or fascination for me (MacLure 2013, 228).

Interestingly, much of the data that shone or sang to me were extracts of personal story and biography that were peculiar to an individual participant. They were the small and very personal stories about the loss of a child at the age of 13, a repeatedly aborted meeting with a Head of School, a colleague's unexpected death and no-one in the university telling the woman's casual colleagues, the casual academic that was told she was 'off-limits' and therefore would not be receiving any future casual teaching, and the story of domestic violence and the need for casual work to financially sustain a family. These stories were not stories repeated by more than one participant or even the most animated in their telling. They were idiosyncratic and defied classification or coding. Additionally, the delivery of these stories in interviews was often very often slow, low in tone, with eyes averted and so would have been missed by my predominantly cognitive method of preserving commonly shared experiences, or those that 'seemed' emotional in their telling. Thus, being affectively open to data intensities allowed me to re-capture many idiosyncratic and deeply personal moments of the women's experience for inclusion in the drama. In addition, including the stories that that g(r)asped me supported Bochner's (2000) request to re-present 'abundant, concrete detail; concern not only for the commonplace, even trivial routines of everyday life, but also for the flesh and blood emotions of people coping with life's contingencies; not only facts but also feelings' (Bochner 2000, 270). Finally, by using my senses in identifying small stories for re-presentation, and not only my analytical mind, allowed me to imbue the restorying process with what Conquergood described as 'energy imagination, and courage… in order not to subsume the sweet, terrible wholeness of life' (1985, 10).

I thus merged the data intensities collated (Ringrose and Renod 2014) with the oft-repeated stories and preoccupations the women had shared, and so by doing I weaved elements of Gee's (2005) holistic process of restorying with a bodily/materialist/non-cognitive approach to selecting stories into a drama in a process yet to be labelled, or 'in-the-making' (Childers et al. 2013).

I next shared the draft script with each of the participants and invited them to comment on the drama and veto any specific story extracts that they did not feel were presented in the context in which they were originally told or that they no longer wanted to share publicly. I also invited the women to attend a dress rehearsal of a performance of the drama as 'It is imperative, both in ethical and practical terms that storytellers are confident their personal experiences will not be exploited, distorted or disparaged in the process of being theatricalised' (Makeham 1998, 170). The women were happy for me to present the script without any further edit or inclusion as they recognised their words and worlds in the drama, and their approval for me to take the script to production offered validation for the promiscuous restorying process with which I'd engaged. I felt both humbled and vindicated. The women who had shared their deeply personal stories with me, had given me authority to share them. I had a responsibility to do so with authenticity and integrity.

CLOSING THOUGHTS

This chapter has afforded me the opportunity to discuss the affordances that arts-informed and drama more specifically offers narrative researchers to re-present the evocation of stories of Others. It has also allowed me to reflect on my resistance to undertaking a narrative analysis with the stories shared by women casual academics. In recognising the resistance, I paused, listening to myself (head and heart) to consider another way of working with the women's narratives. Through this experience I recognise that research plans deviate, and that it is important to heed resistance/s, and to reset our compass to North in order to fulfil the aims of our research. In addition, the chapter has also offered me a chance to discuss my wonder at the stories shared so generously by women casual academics, and the care I took not to slice or dice them, or sm/Other them in the grapholect of academia. Instead, by embracing the outside-ness of being a feminist researcher, I developed a playful and promiscuous 'in-the-making' data restorying process which merges established with 'not-yet-named' restorying processes so that the stories re-presented to an audience could contain 'abundant, concrete detail; concern not only for the commonplace, even trivial routines of everyday life, but also for the flesh and blood emotions of people coping with life's contingencies; not only facts but also feelings' (Bochner 2000, 270). But please don't mistake this chapter as a recipe for 'doing' arts-informed narrative inquiry. I, instead, share with you my reflection/s on the processes I undertook, so that you can feel liberated to follow your own path, so you can feel it's reasonable to pause, or take a detour if you need, all is OK as long as you keep the aims of the research at the centre of all decisions/reactions enacted.

REFERENCES

Arnot, M., & Reay, D. (2007). A Sociology of Pedagogic Voice: Power, Inequality and Pupil Consultation. *Discourse: Studies in the Cultural Politics of Education, 28*(3), 311–325. https://doi.org/10.1080/01596300701458814

Barone, T. E., & Eisner, E. (1997). Arts-Based Educational Research. In R. M. Jaeger (Ed.), *Complementary Methods for Research in Education* (pp. 72–116). Washington, DC: American Education Research Association.

Belenky, M. F., Clinchy, B. M., Goldberger, N. R., & Tarule, J. M. (1986). *Women's Ways of Knowing: The Development of Self, Voice and Mind.* New York: Basic Books.

Bell, J. S. (2002). Narrative Inquiry: More Than Just Telling Stories. *TESOL Quarterly, 36*(2), 207–213. https://doi.org/10.2307/3588331

Bochner, A. P. (2000). Criteria Against Ourselves. *Qualitative Inquiry, 6*(2), 266–272. https://doi.org/10.1177/107780040000600209

Boje, D. M. (1995). Stories of the Storytelling Organization: A Postmodern Analysis of Disney as "Tamara-Land". *The Academy of Management Journal, 38*(4), 997–1035. https://doi.org/10.2307/256618

Bruner, E. M. (1986). Experience and Its Expressions. In V. W. Turner & E. M. Bruner (Eds.), *The Anthropology of Experience* (pp. 3–32). Urbana: University of Illinois Press.

Childers, S. M., Rhee, J.-E., & Daza, S. L. (2013). Promiscuous (Use of) Feminist Methodologies: The Dirty Theory and Messy Practice of Educational Research Beyond Gender. *International Journal of Qualitative Studies in Education, 26*(5), 507–523. https://doi.org/10.1080/09518398.2013.786849

Cole, A. L., & Knowles, G. J. (2008). Arts-Informed Research. In G. J. Knowles & A. L. Cole (Eds.), *Handbook of the Arts in Qualitative Research. Perspectives, Methodologies, Examples and Issues* (pp. 55–70). Los Angeles: Sage.

Connelly, F. M., & Jean Clandinin, D. (1990). Stories of Experience and Narrative Inquiry. *Educational Researcher, 19*(5), 2–1. https://doi.org/10.3102/0013 189X019005002

Conquergood, D. (1985). Performing as a Moral Act: Ethical Dimensions of the Ethnography of Performance. *Literature in Performance, 5*(2), 1–13. https://doi.org/10.1080/10462938509391578

Davis, K., & Skilton-Sylvester, E. (2004). Looking back, taking stock, moving forward: Investigating gender in TESOL. *TESOL Quarterly, 38*(3), 381–404.

Deleuze, G. (1990). *The Logic of Sense* (trans: Lester, M & Stivale, C.). London: The Athlone Press.

Dewey, J. (1934). The Supreme Intellectual Obligation. *Science Education, 18*(1), 1–4. https://doi.org/10.1002/sce.3730180102/full

Diamond, C. T. P., & Mullen, C. A. (1999). The Postmodern Educator. In *Arts-Based Inquiries and Teacher Development*. New York: Peter Lang.

Etherington, K. (2004). *Becoming a Reflexive Researcher: Using Our Selves in Research.* London: Jessica Kingsley Publishers.

Ewing, R., & Hughes, J. (2008). Arts-Informed Inquiry in Teacher Education: Contesting the Myths. *European Educational Research Journal, 7*(4), 512–522. https://doi.org/10.2304/eerj.2008.7.4.512

Fleckenstein, K. S. (1996). Images, Words, and Narrative Epistemology. *College English, 58*(8), 914–933. http://www.jstor.org/stable/378229

Gallese, V., & Wojciehowski, H. (2011). How Stories Make Us Feel: Toward an Embodied Narratology. *California Italian Studies, 2*(1), 1–38. http://www.escholarship.org/uc/item/3jg726c2. Accessed 1 Oct 2017.

Gee, J. P. (2005). *An Introduction to Discourse Analysis: Theory and Method* (2nd ed.). London: Routledge.

Gibson, J. (2011). Saying It Right: Creating Ethical Verbatim Theatre. *NEO: Journal for Higher Degree Students in the Social Sciences and Humanities, 4*, 1–18. http://www.arts.mq.edu.au/documents/hdr_journal_neo/neoJanet2011_2.pdf. Accessed 1 Oct 2017.

Gilligan, C. (1982). *In a Different Voice.* Cambridge: Harvard University Press.

Gould, S. (1996). *The mismeasure of man.* New York: W.W. Norton.

Gubrium, J. F., & Holstein, J. A. (2002). *Handbook of Interview Research: Context & Method Politics & Gender.* Thousand Oaks: Sage.

Harding, S. (1987). Introduction: Is There a Feminist Method? In S. Harding (Ed.), *Feminism and Methodology: Social Science Issues* (pp. 1–14). Bloomington: Indiana University Press.

Hardy, B. (1968). Towards a Poetics of Fiction: 3) an Approach through Narrative. *NOVEL: A Forum on Fiction, 2*(1), 5–14. https://doi.org/10.2307/1344792

Hendry, P. M. (2010). Narrative as inquiry. *The Journal of Educational Research, 103*(2), 72–80. https://doi.org/10.1080/00220670903323354

Hesse-Biber, S. N., Leavy, P., & Yaiser, M. L. (2004). Feminist Approaches to Research as a Process: Reconceptualizing Epistemology, Methodology and Method. In S. N. Hesse-Biber & M. L. Yaiser (Eds.), *Feminist Perspectives on Social Research* (pp. 3–26). New York: Oxford University Press.

Jones, K. (2004). Minimalist Passive Interviewing Technique and Team Analysis of Narrative Qualitative Data. In F. Rapport (Ed.), *New Qualitative Methodologies in Health and Social Care* (pp. 35–54). London: Routledge.

Knowles, J. G., & Cole, A. L. (Eds.). (2008). *Handbook of the Arts in Qualitative Research: Perspectives, Methodologies, Examples, and Issues.* Thousand Oaks: Sage.

Kramp, M. K. (2004). Exploring Life and Experience Through Narrative Inquiry. In K. de Marrais & S. D. Lapan (Eds.), *Foundations for Research: Methods of Inquiry in Education and the Social Sciences* (pp. 103–121). Mahwah: Lawrence Erlbaum Associates Publishers.

Langer, S. K. (1942). *Philosophy in a New Key.* Cambridge: Harvard University Press.

Langer, S. K. (1962). *Philosophical Sketches.* Baltimore: Johns Hopkins University Press.

Lather, P. (2006). Paradigm Proliferation as a Good Thing to Think with: Teaching Research in Education as a Wild Profusion. *International Journal of Qualitative Studies in Education, 19*(1), 35–57. https://doi.org/10.1080/09518390500450144

Lieblich, A. (2006). Vicissitudes: A Study, a Book, a Play: Lessons from the Work of a Narrative Scholar. *Qualitative Inquiry, 12*(1), 60–80. https://doi.org/10.1177/1077800405282795

Lugones, M. C., Spelman, E. V., Lugones, M. C., & Spelman, E. V. (1983). Have We Got a Theory for You! Feminist Theory, Cultural Imperialism and the Demand for 'the Woman's Voice'. *Women's Studies International Forum, 6*(6), 573–581. https://doi.org/10.1016/0277-5395(83)90019-5

MacLure, M. (2013). The Wonder of Data. *Cultural Studies ↔ Critical Methodologies, 13*(4), 228–232. https://doi.org/10.1177/1532708613487863

Makeham, P. (1998). Community Stories: Aftershocks and Community Theatre. In V. Kelly (Ed.), *Our Australian Theatre in the 1990s* (pp. 168–181). Amsterdam: Rodopi.

Merleau-Ponty, M. (1962). *Phenomenology of Perception.* London: Routledge.

Merriam, S. B., Caffarella, R. S., & Baumgartner, L. M. (2007). *Learning in Adulthood: A Comprehensive Guide* (3rd ed.). San Francisco: Jossey-Bass.

Nissen, N. (2011). Challenging Perspectives: Women, Complementary and Alternative Medicine, and Social Change. *Interface, 3*(2), 187–212. http://www.interfacejournal.net/wordpress/wp-content/uploads/2011/12/Interface-3-2-Nissen.pdf

Pagis, M. (2009). Embodied Self-Reflexivity. *Social Psychology Quarterly, 72*(3), 265–283. https://doi.org/10.1177/019027250907200308

Richards, J. C. (2011). 'Every Word Is True': Stories of Our Experiences in a Qualitative Research Course. *The Qualitative Report, 16*(3), 782–819. http://www.nova.edu/ssss/QR/QR16-3/richards.pdf. Accessed 1 Oct 2017.

Richardson, L. (2000). Writing: A Method of Inquiry. In N. K. Denzin & Y. S. Lincoln (Eds.), *Handbook of Qualitative Research* (pp. 923–948). Thousand Oaks: Sage.

Ringrose, J., & Renold, E. (2014). 'F**K Rape!': Exploring Affective Intensities in a Feminist Research Assemblage. *Qualitative Inquiry, 20*(6), 772–780. https://doi.org/10.1177/1077800414530261

Sikes, P., & Gale, K. (2006). *Narrative Approaches to Education Research*. Plymouth: University of Plymouth.

Wake, C. (2010). Towards a Working Definition of Verbatim Theatre. In P. Brown (Ed.), *Verbatim: Staging Memory and Community* (pp. 2–5). Strawberry Hills: Currency Press.

Wake, C. (2013). To Witness Mimesis: The Politics, Ethics, and Aesthetics of Testimonial Theatre in Through the Wire 1. *Modern Drama, 56*(1), 102–125. https://doi.org/10.1353/mdr.2013.0009

The Philosophical, Ethical and Political Considerations Involved in Theatricalising Data

Abstract Responding to Mazzei and Jackson's (Introduction: the limit of voice. In: Jackson A, Mazzei L (ed) Voice in qualitative inquiry: challenging conventional, interpretative, and critical conceptions in qualitative research. Routledge, London, 1–13, 2009) advice to feminist researchers to democratise research by fully exposing all decision-making processes, I make transparent the philosophical, ethical and political considerations which informed my decision to employ proto-verbatim theatre to re-present the lived experience of women casual academics. In particular, I contemplate the role of Brechtian and feminist theatre in creating highly theatricalised verbatim theatre to evocatively engage an audience, and to make transparent the *re*-telling nature of research communication. I finally propose that the conceptual research framework we adopt ought to lay the foundation for *all* creative decisions made in an Arts-based research, to create research cohesion and integrity.

Keywords Arts-based research • Brecht • Feminist research • Feminist theatre • Transparency of communication • Verbatim drama

Central to this chapter is Mazzei and Jackson's (2009) advice to feminist researchers to democratise research by fully exposing all decision-making processes. This seems especially important when the research involves re-presenting the voices of Others. In this chapter, I therefore make

© The Author(s) 2018   45
G. Crimmins, *Theatricalising Narrative Research on Women
Casual Academics*, Palgrave Studies in Gender and Education,
https://doi.org/10.1007/978-3-319-71562-9_4

transparent the philosophical, ethical and political considerations which informed my decision to employ a particular form of drama (proto-verbatim theatre) when re-presenting the lived experience of women casual academics. I offer considerations and musings on my practice that are consciously transferable to other forms of Arts-based research, as all forms of communication embody power relations, offer affordances and limitations to participants, and reflect philosophies and discourses.

In particular, I contemplate whether privileging dramatic, neat and coherent narrative structures potentially silences the perceived realities of storytellers and their stories, and further Others the stories that fall outside of orderly and recognisable patterns of representation. I also ponder whether a mimetic performance aesthetic within a naturalistic dramatic structure serves to propagate the idea of an inescapable and unalterable causality, which may serve to reinforce unequal social orders and potentially foster fatalism. Latterly, I consider how a highly theatricalised form of verbatim theatre, based on an aestheticised representation of the words and expression of participants, may be used to evocatively engage an audience with/in a deliberately transparent, though complex, form of narrative re-presentation.

These considerations are presented to explain why I chose to restory participants' narratives into a sub-genre of verbatim drama with a heightened aesthetic, called proto-verbatim. Proto-verbatim is a sub-genre of verbatim which makes use of the 'real words' gathered from those being represented, re-presented in a highly aestheticised form (Duggan 2013), and employs rigorous research processes and principle. Yet, more generally, in this chapter I seek to demonstrate that all communication genre inhabit (and so either reinforce or resist) dominant philosophical and political positions. When engaging in Arts-based research we must therefore consider carefully the ethics entwined with/in the forms of communication we employ, both aesthetically and politically. Moreover, I consider that the philosophical and methodological stance we adopt for a project ought to lay the foundation for all creative decisions made in an Arts-based research project and if we make all decisions based on who we are, what we believe in, and what we want to achieve with/in our research, our projects will be cohesive and we, as researchers, will maintain our academic integrity.

As discussed in Chap. 1 Bhabha (1990) suggests that a nation shapes and narrates itself through the stories it tells, and I suggested that if the stories of casualisation currently told is recounted in weights and measures, then the shape of our narrative is hollow and lacks guts. So, in contrast to a gutless telling of the experience of women casual academics, I sought to capture and communicate women's embodied stories through performance – replete with breathing, moving speaking bodies. I also reflected (in Chap. 3) on the capacity of drama to incorporate large sections of research participants' stories, uncut or sliced into bitesize pieces, in order to share the detail and nuance of storied experience. I build on these ideas in this chapter as I describe the merits of verbatim drama as a form through which the lived experience of women casual academics can be re-presented, and so first offer an overview of the verbatim genre.

Verbatim Drama

Verbatim drama is a form of documentary drama whose texts develop from stories unearthed by a researcher/dramatist. This process contrasts with traditional processes of playwriting where a writer constructs a drama text out of her/his pre-existing ideas and predetermined aims. The verbatim drama develops out of everyday people's conversation and perspective (Paget 1987). Early verbatim dramas tended to focus on the financial hardship caused to communities by the closure of the factories and heavy industry, which had been the livelihood and lifeblood of many regions in the UK (Andersen and Wilkinson 2007). They were generally presented in non-traditional performance spaces and provided a platform for the silent or marginalised people within communities (Wake 2010). The main aim of verbatim theatre was to capture and feed-back the life stories and oral history of and to a local community in a bid to build community and empowerment (Paget 1987). In line with John Berger's (1990) consideration that a people or a class which fails to tell and capture its story has less agency to act than a people that can situate itself in history, so verbatim theatre is a political art form that seeks to capture and re-present stories to support community cohesion and provoke community agency.

It was verbatim's power 'to help cohere, to create communitas, to function as a means of embodied thinking through contexts and problems' (Duggan and Peschel 2016) that excited me and drew me to the genre. It bid me to explore more of its potentialities.

All Stories Are Mediated

Yet, we need to take care when we re-present Others' stories that we don't re-present them as if they are an unmediated objective account of a truth, as 'facts', or as a transparent mediation of people's lived experience, as all told stories are mediated, and especially so when a story we tell is second hand (Guttorm 2012; Minh-ha and Bourdier 1982; Minh-ha 1989).

Stories are constructed and told through the perspective of the teller, and encase the *meaning* of an experience, though not necessarily a 'truth'. I am reminded of Wang and Geale's (2015) consideration that the 'purpose of narrative inquiry is to reveal the meanings of the individual's experiences as opposed to objective, decontextualized truths' (p. 196). I am reminded that the story reveals subjective realities and remembrances of the teller within her/his social context, and we as researchers hear a story according to our understanding of the world, framed within and by our social context.

It's likely then, that the storytelling and re-telling process is a little like the children's game 'Chinese Whispers' (as it is known in the UK, or 'Telephone' in France and the US) where story events, characters, and lines shift, morph or disappear in the telling, hearing and re-telling experience. The story told to us reverberates through and in us as matter, and the story we re-tell in response is one that 'matters' to us, as our interpretation of the heard and felt experience. Our re-tellings are thus refractions of the stories we hear and feel (Fig. 4.1).

Fig. 4.1   Refractions

Our re-tellings are refractions of the stories we hear and feel.
Acknowledging our role in the refraction process when we re-present Others' words and experience to participants and audiences, therefore, is ethically important. The participants whose stories we co-author, and the audiences who offer 'listening ears' (Wake 2010) to our co-constructed stories deserve to know that we as researchers/artists, have 'translated' and transmuted the stories we re-tell.

A third important consideration in re-presenting the stories of women casual academics is/was the emotional investment it takes/took to centralise the communication of Others. Women casual academics are Othered by nature of their sex (de Beauvoir 1949 in McCann and Kim 2003) and in relation to their peripheral status, and lack of voice and presence in university (Brown et al. 2010). Consequently, I do/did not want to Other them further by speaking *of* or *for* them (Alcoff 2006, 2009). Yet at the same time I am/was aware that it is impossible to know another (Alcoff 2006; Richardson 1997), or neutrally re-present anOther (Richardson 1997). Consequently, re-presenting Others is a translation or re-telling. I therefore identify/identified that the most significant challenge in the restorying process, and indeed in the entire project, is/was to find a balance between centralising the stories and voices of women casual academics whilst explicitly exposing the constructed nature of its/my re-presentation. The emotional toll of this challenge is accepted by Josselson who claimed that researchers should carry out narrative research 'in anguish' as 'we balance the vulnerability of the participants with the need to retain the personal nature of the narrative for it to be of value to others' (Josselson 1996, 70).

This notion required me to contemplate how I would re-present the narratives of women casual academics in a way that makes explicit the re-constructed nature of narrative data, and I was provoked, in particular, to consider whether verbatim theatre co support me to do so. I therefore sought insight from theatre scholars and practitioners.

THE BROAD SPECTRUM OF VERBATIM

Wake (2010) suggests that verbatim theatre represents a broad spectrum of sub-genres, each encompassing different aesthetics and specific artistic/ political intent and Little (n.d.) describes it an encompassing genre that at one end of its spectrum sit 'hyper-aestheticised productions... whilst at the other end sit productions where practitioners inadvertently drain the drama from theatrical representation in attempting to preserve a perceived 'truth' (Little n.d., n.p.). Indeed, examples of verbatim theatre present a vastly varied scope of theatre scope for entertainment and theatrical metaphor to mimetic representation and 'reproduction' of past event. For the British dramatist David Hare the crafting a verbatim drama is an art from, and for whom the 'driftwood' of a narrative is there to be found, though requires carving and painting 'to make art' (Hare 2005). Similarly, Max Stafford-Clark, an acclaimed theatre director, suggests that a documentary play ought to contain a theatrical metaphor (Hammond and Steward 2008). Thus, for Hare and Stafford-Clark the production of a verbatim play involves the creative and artistic manipulation and fabrication of verbatim material in order to create engaging and metaphoric theatre. They will happily add fictionalised characters and events to stories gathered from community in order to help create dramatic cohesion and impact. Yet, theatre practitioners Alecky Blythe, Hilary Halba and Stuart Young ask actors in their verbatim productions to wear headphones throughout the performance, through which they receive the digital recording of the interview of the person they are re-presenting, in an attempt to re-recite and re-create the speech patterns and words they hear with absolute precision (Hammond and Steward 2008). Their use of headphones represents an attempt to prevent aestheticizing contributor's testimony with heightened performances or theatrical mystique (Hammond and Steward 2008).

This cursory examination of two approaches to verbatim highlight the differing theatrical positions that theatre, and all art forms, embody. They offer a basis for me to consider in more detail the theatrical, political and ethical preoccupations which informed my decision to employ a particular form of verbatim theatre (proto-verbatim) to re-present the stories of women casual academics. The considerations include the role of fictionalisation of Others' testimonies and the limitations of muted theatricality and mimetic performance.

The Fictionalisation of Others' Testimonies

Some researchers, playwrights and directors 'fictionalise' content within a verbatim drama in order to create consistent characterisations, coherent 'neat' narrative development, or to make a political or social statement; others de/select participant interview material based exclusively on its 'dramatic appeal'; whilst others still, fail to involve participants in the shaping of the drama by simply taking testimonies and crafting a drama according to their own interpretation of the 'data'. Such playmakers have been criticised for manipulating verbatim material and potentially further silencing the voiceless participants. For instance, theatre historian and scholar Derek Paget describes plays that over-rely on fictional characters and narratives as 'quasi-verbatim' (Forsyth and Megson 2009) and Little (n.d.) notes that the practice of only re-presenting episodes and details of dramatic appeal whilst ignoring the smaller stories of everydayness 'exploit and manipulate source material in the interests of spectacle, aesthetic appeal and audience engagement' (Little n.d.). More specifically, Polkinghorne (1995) suggested that story depth and detail are necessary to understand experience, that memories conveyed as stories retain the complexity of the situation in which the event took place, and reflect the emotional and motivational meanings associated with it. So, editing out such detail and seeming 'inconsequence' in the re-telling process potentially removes the complexity, messiness and meaning of the storied experience. Indeed, Heddon (2008, 128) notes that a lack of negotiation and consultation within the restorying process has led some scholars to describe verbatim as 'theatre of solicitation or appropriation'.

Yet, more specifically, Wake (2013), suggests that when a writer or dramatist omits someone's story from a play altogether, it results in a sort of double silencing, where the artist solicits a story from a silenced subject only to silence them once again. Finally, it is thought that when the interviews and stories of contributors are ignored, edited, and merged with fiction, without consultation and negotiation with participants, 'the silenced and traumatised are silenced and traumatised again... and the rhetoric of the social and political efficacy of verbatim theatre becomes empty' (Gibson 2011, 12).

Pause.

Gibson's words are powerful. They arrest (me). They remind me of the damage well-meaning researcher/artists can do. They remind me that we must first do no harm.

Pause.

The perspectives discussed above illuminate some important considerations for Arts-based researchers. For instance, it appears ethically important to let participants and audiences know that the re-presentation is an artistic *translation* of gathered stories, and to make it explicit if any fictionalised material has been created and woven in to the re-presentation. It also invites us to reflect on the importance of engaging with participants in the 'shaping' process of the artistic form of communication.

These reflections persuaded me to employ only the participants' words and expressions, to make explicit to an audience any deviation from this practice, and to liaise regularly with research participants when I was scripting and theatricalising their stories so that they could contribute ideas and check that I was re-presenting their stories ethically and with verisimilitude.

THE LIMITATIONS OF MUTED THEATRICALITY AND MIMETIC PERFORMANCE

A second key consideration with which I engaged was the notion that arts practitioners who fail to fully utilise the aesthetic potential of a chosen genre might show a disservice to research participants, and fail to transparently communicate their role as artist/translator in the presentation of the work. For instance, it is said that whilst a mimetic physical and aural reproduction of Others' words and actions may reflect an ethical attempt to privilege the detailed vocal and physical print of research participants, the technique's theatrical value is often limited (Little n.d.). By choosing 'non-interference' the practitioners may deny the participants their ability to use their artistic skills and theatre's capacity to engage, inform and cohere audiences to its full capacity (Little n.d.). In addition, attempts to reproduce the voice print and physicality of participants can lend itself to a performance aesthetic based on mimesis, an acting form which aims to deny or submerge the constructedness of the theatre event by privileging the life-likeness of characters and the inevitability of action.

A particular critique that is offered against a mimetic performance aesthetic is that it is predicated on and promotes false notions of a dramatist's 'objectivity' and an ability to create a 'faithful' rendering of Others' existence. Indeed, realistic and naturalistic genres of drama that promote mimetic performance have been critiqued for upholding a 'deluded objectivity' and outdated ontology (Erikson 2009). Correspondingly, a mimetic performance in alliance with a causal dramatic structure (where A leads to B, which leads to C) is said to normalise and reinforce an unequal established social order and extol an epistemology of inescapable and unalterable causality (Sierz 2000). It's also suggested that all actions that are represented naturalistically on stage reflect the politically reckless notion that those actions are 'natural' and lead to necessary and predictable outcomes (Sierz 2000). Further, Gibson (2011, 2) suggests that attempts to truthfully reproduce and represent Others' stories 'that have as their base a notion of fidelity to some original or authentic source' are naive as they deny the constructed nature of verbatim narrative and ultimately reinforce the power relationship between the contributor and the re-teller. Gibson continues that verbatim theatre presents 'many layers of removal and interpretation from the original source material' (Gibson 2011, 5) and theatre artists who claim to 'truthfully' or objectively represent Others' stories fail to identify the personal constructedness of their theatrical renderings.

The criticisms that have been laid against 'quasi-verbatim' (Forsyth and Megson 2009) fictionalised, and mimetic 'realistic' forms of dramatic communication highlight that all communication genre contain ontological and therefore political positions. Consequently, Squiers (2012) suggests that practitioners need to employ theatrical aesthetics that are in alignment with their ontological and political positions and the specific aims of their theatrical project. That is, how we express academic research is ever neutral. Every communication form – including every artistic genre and subgenre – inhabit a particular philosophical, ethical and political stance. It is therefore incumbent upon us to consider the philosophical and political implications reflected in the art forms we intend to employ if we are to engage positively impactful Arts-based educational research.

As a result of the insights drawn from theatre critics and scholars' discussions (relating to of the limitations of various translations or forms of verbatim drama, including fictionalised 'quasi verbatim' and mimetic reconstructions of Others' stories) I felt compelled to investigate other styles of verbatim drama along the verbatim continuum in a bid to find a form that would allow me to transparently re-present and engage an audience in the stories of women causal academics in Australia. This discussion aligns with the main aim of this monograph – to present 'a personal tale of what went on in the backstage of doing research' (Ellis and Bochner 2000, 741), but also reflects the praxis in Arts-based educational research processes.

HIGHLY THEATRICALISED VERBATIM THEATRE

Verbatim drama occupies a spectrum between reality and fiction (Hammond and Steward 2008) and in contrast to the mimesis of realistic and naturalism, some theatre artists create highly aestheticised forms of verbatim which use the actual expressions of participations whilst seeking to mediate 'the essence' instead of the actuality of contributor experience (Beck 2013). These latter artists attempt to reveal the mechanics of their theatrical staging by translating source material in the forms of drama, dance, image or song to express spoken testimony and make explicit the playwrights' authorship of the drama (Gibson 2011). Beck (2013) suggests that highly theatricalised verbatim drama which reacts against the theatrical limitations of mimesis and privileges aesthetic communication is distinct from traditional verbatim so is best described as a sub-genre or 'post-verbatim'. Yet the notion that highly aestheticised verbatim is 'post' is contested on the grounds that theatre practitioners have been aestheticizing reported narrative and documentary for many decades, and that perhaps labelling the process as 'post' locates the dramatic genre into a late twentieth and early twenty-first philosophical and theatrical milieu. For the purposes of easy classification then, I refer to verbatim drama that communicates the idea that truth and experience are personally and transiently constructed and that a telling of Others' experience is inevitably a re-telling by demonstrating the constructedness of the text as highly theatricalised verbatim theatre. Such theatre is also said to privilege audience experience over mimetic realism (Wake 2013). In practice, highly theatricalised verbatim aims to heighten, illuminate, and amplify the essence of the lived experience of contributors, and 'brings to the surface for the audience's consideration what cannot always be articulated in words' (Beck 2013, 142).

Aestheticised verbatim also recognises the role of art in making strange or unfamiliar that which is often camouflaged by its ordinary everyday exterior. Seemingly ordinary everydayness causes bias and prevents us from easily seeing in other ways or 'seeing otherwise'. Alice Fulton's (2001) evocative poetry helps us to understand this:

> Because truths we don't suspect have a hard time making themselves felt, as when thirteen species of whiptail lizards composed entirely of females stay undiscovered due to bias against such things existing, we have to meet the universe halfway. Nothing will unfold for us unless we move toward what looks like to us like nothing: faith is a cascade. The sky's high solid is anything but...

And for me, the normalisation of casualisation of academia is anything but..., and women casual academics being reduced to number and percentage requires us to see and show anew.

One particular form of highly theatricalised verbatim theatre is known as 'proto-verbatim'. Proto-verbatim appears to be distinctive as it makes use of the 'real words' gathered from those being represented, re-presented in a highly aestheticised form (Duggan 2013) and employs rigorous research processes and principles. Proto-verbatim makers do not fabricate scenes or characters yet make manifest the constructedness of the theatre event through the use of post-Brechtian theatre conventions such as direct address to the audience, stark white lightening, and the use of tableaux/ frozen image. In particular, Duggan (2013) suggests that the deliberate and overt presentation of theatre conventions makes much more transparent, and therefore more authentic and ethical, the re-presentational nature of verbatim theatre than a production that hides its constructedness (Duggan 2013). In addition, proto-verbatim amalgamates techniques of overt theatre constructedness designed for an audience to dispassionately analyse social structures and oppression within the narrative, with dramatic elements such as naturalistic characterisation designed to engage an audience's emotional connection with the characters presented. The amalgamation is designed to awaken an audience cognitively, politically and emotionally, compelling them/us to think, feel and act.

Highly theatricalised-verbatim generally and proto-verbatim more specifically, employ many aesthetic conventions from political and feminist theatre which align with the philosophical foundation and aims of this project.

VERBATIM THEATRE AS A POLITICAL ART FORM

The founder of the Scottish popular theatre company 7:84, John McGrath, argued 'the theatre can never "cause" a social change, but it can act politically to articulate pressure towards one, help people celebrate their strengths and maybe build their self-confidence... above all, it can be the way people find their voice and their collective determination' (McGrath 1981, p. xxvii). Correspondingly, most verbatim theatre is described as politically motivated (Heddon 2008) as it intends to 'give voice to the voiceless' in society (Heddon 2008, 128), offer 'faceness' to the faceless' (Wake 2013), and 'gives listening ears to the voices that often go unheard' (Wake 2010, 3). And Hesford argues that 'one of the standards against which political theatre is judged is whether a performance shakes audiences out of complacency' (Hesford 2005, 104–105).

Seeing strange the everyday is considered a central characteristic of political theatre. Hesford considers mimetic performances that merely elicit a sense of identification and empathetic alignment with character undermines the opportunity for audiences to be politically shaken or motivated towards political thought, discussion or action. For Sontag, the arousal of sympathy alone simply reflects and reinforces an audience's impotence, and fails to incite political consciousness-raising or motivate political action (Hesford 2005). Therefore, although there are many different strands of political theatre most political theatre avoids the hegemony of realistic drama aesthetic and the mimetic reproductions of events or characters (Sierz 2000). In accordance with these ideas I chose to avoid a purely mimetic performance aesthetic and causal dramatic structure in a bid for my audience to desist on seeing the sky's high as solid (Fulton 2001) or women casual academics as number and percentage.

PROTO-VERBATIM INHABITS MANY OF THE POLITICAL AND AESTHETIC CHARACTERISTICS OF FEMINIST THEATRE

Like political theatre, the concept of 'feminist theatre' is difficult to contain within one definition as it embodies a variety of political perspectives that relate to theatre in many different ways. However, generally speaking, 'feminists involved in the creation or analysis of [feminist] theatre usually wish to enact, embody or inspire some kind of political, personal or cultural change via the public platform of theatre' (Tarker n.d.). In particular, feminist theatre identifies that traditional western theatre tends to focus on white male protagonists, who represent a fixed and singular identity. Such structures are said to perpetuate 'a masculine perspective of the world at the expense of the feminine' (Tarker n.d.). In response/resistance feminist theatre often employs episodic dramatic structures with multiple protagonists in an attempt to subvert the Aristotelian aesthetic of privileging a single protagonist, and a linear and teleological plot complete with resolution. Indeed, most feminist theatre features an ensemble of women and juxtaposes, within non-linear dramatic episodes, multiple women's experience. Moreover, it generally avoids the representation of interpersonal conflict leading to climax and easy resolution favouring instead a juxtaposition of characters and their stories. This way a variety of women's experiences are expressed and a series of perspectives sit alongside one another to create dialectic and reject the dichotomisation of stances which connotes a right and wrong, a truth and a falsehood.

Feminist theatrical structures acknowledge that each woman's stories matter, and deserve to be heard. In performance, feminist theatre is characterised by ensemble-based acting and a presentational aesthetic where song, image or tableaux are employed to undermine mimesis and illuminate the social and political social relations represented in the narrative.

Feminist theatre is made by women about women, with the aim of creating artistic and aesthetic work based on the lives of women and is often focused on societal re/structure. Patti Gillespie argued that the primary aim of feminist theatre is 'action, not art' (Goodman 1993, 32), and that it is characterised by women taking ownership of the means of production. That is, women in feminist theatre adopt the traditionally male roles of writer, director and technician in an attempt to subvert traditional theatre enterprise where historically women have been denied power in the theatre apparatus (Diamond 1998). The feminist theatre collective thus becomes a microcosm of an alternative societal structure (Diamond 1998).

THEATRE, AND ART IN GENERAL, CAN SHOW US AN 'OTHERWISE'

As Reinelt observed (2009) from a woman's perspective the personal is political and as such the personal needs to be re-presented in public, so feminist theatre dismantles the division between private and public concerns and in doing so creates a new dramaturgy to reflect women's ways of knowing and being in society. As Brown (1995) argued, women identify truth and experience as subjectively and emotionally constructed. The theatrical exposure of women's truth and experience therefore needs a theatrical form that accommodates and expresses women's emotion (Brown 1995). Finally, 'since women's subordination is partly achieved through the construction and positioning of us as private – sexual, familial, emotional... then the voicing of women's experience acquires an inherently confessional cast' (Brown 1995, 42). Consequently, feminist theatre, especially contemporary feminist theatre, tends to develop collaborative, confessional and emotionally expressive dramatisation of multiple women's/women characters' personal and social experience and perspective.

Thus theatre, and art more specifically, reflects ideologies and values
Art is not, never was, never can be, neutral

How and with whom we make art and what and who our art focuses upon,
either supports or seeks to subvert social structures
Art is emblazoned with political statement
As George Orwell claimed (2005/1946), the opinion that art should have
nothing to do with politics is itself a political statement.

I share a detailed discussion around the specific theatricalising processes I adopted to restory the narratives shared by six women casual academics in Chap. 6 but describe below an overview of the elements of political, feminist and proto-verbatim which informed my script development process. I do this to demonstrate the relationship between theory and practice, to share what I now understand about the philosophical, ethical and political implications of various artistic aesthetics, and to allow you to see behind the scenes of the creations of a drama out of narrative data.

For instance, the criticisms laid against fabricating narratives, mimesis, and causal structures informed my commitment to adopt a highly theatricalised verbatim approach to re-presenting the lived experience of women casual academics based only on the words spoken by the women participants. I also sought to present emotionally arresting moments of dramatic action in order to capture an audience's affective engagement with the women characters. And I chose to employ an episodic structure to resist the notion of inevitable causality and destiny.

The structures of feminist theatre also motivated me to followed Dostoevsky's 'dialogical principle' of drama development (Bakhtin 1986) which accommodates multiple characters, perspectives and voices, as they relate to and interact with each other. Further, dialogical plot lines conflate causal narrative structures which purport an inevitability and dissuade audience's from critically seeing how things can and might be otherwise consequently promoting political lethargy and stasis.

I sought to make transparent the translated/refracted nature of verbatim drama by drawing attention to the constructedness of the theatre event by presenting stage lights on stage, employing direct address to the audience, punctuating scenes with scene titles and a tableau, and using a chorus figure to comment upon, in song, the action of each scene. I rejected focusing on a single protagonist/subject by paying attention to multiple women characters' stories and experiences.

CLOSING CONSIDERATIONS

As I identified at the beginning of this chapter, Mazzei and Jackson's (2009) urged feminist researchers to democratise the research process by opening to others all our research decisions. In response I have shared with you the philosophical, ethical and political considerations that informed my decision to employ a proto-verbatim drama as a form of research communication to re-present the lived experience of women casual academics. I discussed that theatre – or any other medium of communication – is never neutral and consider that when choosing to adopt an artistic genre through which to present unearthed data or narratives, the choice of aesthetic ought to align with, and embody y/our philosophical, ethical and political understanding. Alignment between form, content and intent is therefore central to the integrity of Arts-based research.

More specifically, I mused that:

As our entireties and emergences do not fit neatly into boxes and tables,
our story currently told,
recounted in weights and measures
lacks breath, and guts,
so we (women casual academics) are yet to be voiced.

We need to tell our own story,
an embodied story,
to cohere, to create communitas.

I gather stories from Others like me,
and the stories reverberate and crash/meld into my story,
I know in my re-telling, I refract mine-and-Others' lived moments.

I choose to re-tell our stories in embodied performance, verbatim
Not one but many women's stories.
I tear apart the well-made-play of fate and fatalism, of male heroism
I expose the seams of the dress to show how it has been made,
Every stitch threaded with philosophical and political intent

The research is dressed
Ready to show an 'Other'wise story

REFERENCES

Alcoff, L. M. (2006). *Visible Identities: Race, Gender, and the Self.* New York: Oxford University Press.

Alcoff, L. M. (2009). The Problem of Speaking for Others. In A. Y. Jackson & L. A. Mazzei (Eds.), *Voice in Qualitative Inquiry: Challenging Conventional, Interpretive, and Critical Conceptions in Qualitative Research* (pp. 117–135). London: Routledge.

Anderson, M., & Wilkinson, L. (2007). A Resurgence of Verbatim Theatre: Authenticity, Empathy and Transformation. *Australasian Drama Studies, 50,* 153–169. https://www.questia.com/library/journal/1P3-1285304751/a-resurgence-of-verbatim-theatre-authenticity-empathy. Accessed 6 Oct 2017.

Bakhtin, M. M. (1986). The Problem of Speech Genres. In C. Emerson & M. Holquist (Eds.), *Speech Genres and Other Late Essays.* Austin: University of Texas Press.

Beck, S. (2013). Playing War: Encountering Soldiers and Navigating Ethical Responsibilities in the Creation of Black Watch. *International Journal of Scottish Theatre and Screen, 6*(1), 131–153. http://journals.qmu.ac.uk/index.php/IJOSTS/article/viewFile/168/pdf_1

Berger, J. (1990). *Ways of Seeing.* New York: Penguin Books.

Bhabha, H. K. (1990). *Nation and Narration.* London: Routledge.

Brown, W. (1995). *States of Injury: Power and Freedom in Late Modernity* (Vol. 120). Princeton: Princeton University Press.

Brown, T., Goodman, J., & Yasukawa, K. (2010). Academic Casualization in Australia: Class Divisions in the University. *Journal of Industrial Relations, 52*(2), 169–182. https://doi.org/10.1177/0022185609359443

Diamond, E. (1998). *Unmaking Mimesis: Essays on Feminism and Theatre.* London/New York: Routledge.

Duggan, P. (2013). Others, Spectatorship, and the Ethics of Verbatim Performance. *New Theatre Quarterly, 29*(2), 146–158. https://doi.org/10.1017/s0266464x13000250

Duggan, P., & Peschel, L. (2016). *Performing (for) Survival.* Hampshire: Palgrave Macmillan.

Ellis, C., & Bochner, A. P. (2000). Autoethnography, Personal Narrative, Reflexivity: Researcher as Subject. In N. K. Denzin & Y. S. Lincoln (Eds.), *The Handbook of Qualitative Research* (pp. 733–768). Thousand Oaks: Sage.

Erickson, J. (2009). On Mimesis (and Truth) in Performance. *Journal of Dramatic Theory and Criticism, 23*(2), 21–38. https://journals.ku.edu/index.php/jdtc/article/view/4362/4090

Forsyth, A., & Megson, C. (2009). *Get Real: Documentary Theatre Past and Present.* Hampshire: Palgrave Macmillan.

Fulton, A. (2001). *Powers of Congress: Poems.* Louisville: Sarabande Books.

Gibson, J. (2011). Saying It Right: Creating Ethical Verbatim Theatre. *NEO: Journal for Higher Degree Students in the Social Sciences and Humanities,* 4, 1–18. http://www.arts.mq.edu.au/documents/hdr_journal_neo/neoJa-net2011_2.pdf

Goodman, L. (1993). *Contemporary Feminist Theatres: To Each Her Own.* London: Routledge.

Guttorm, H. E. (2012). Becoming-(a)-Paper, or an Article Undone: (Post-) Knowing and Writing (Again), Nomadic and So Messy. *Qualitative Inquiry,* 18(7), 595–605. https://doi.org/10.1177/1077800412450157

Hammond, W., & Steward, D. (Eds.). (2008). *Verbatim: Contemporary Documentary Theatre.* London, UK: Oberon Books.

Hare, D. (2005). *Obedience, Struggle and Revolt.* London: Faber and Faber.

Heddon, D. (2008). *Autobiography and Performance.* Basingstoke: Palgrave Macmillan.

Hesford, W. (2005). Rhetorical Memory, Political Theater, and the Traumatic Present. *Transformations,* 16(2), 104–117. http://www.catherinefilloux.com/articles/Hesford1.pdf

Josselson, R. (1996). *Ethics and Process in the Narrative Study of Lives* (1st ed.). Thousand Oaks: Sage Publications.

Little, S. (n.d.). In and out of tune with reality: Opposed strategies of documentary theatre. *Double Dialogues,* 14. http://www.doubledialogues.com/article/the-politics-of-avarice-re-visiting-roger-halls-sharemarket-comedies/. Accessed 6 Oct 2017.

Mazzei, L. A., & Jackson, A. Y. (2009). Introduction: The Limit of Voice. In A. Jackson & L. Mazzei (Eds.), *Voice in Qualitative Inquiry: Challenging Conventional, Interpretative, and Critical Conceptions in Qualitative Research* (pp. 1–13). London: Routledge.

McCann, C., & Kim, S.-K. (2003). *Feminist Theory Reader: Local and Global Perspectives.* New York: Routledge.

McGrath, J. (1981). *A Good Night Out: Popular Theatre: Audience, Class and Form.* London: Nick Hern Books.

Minh-ha, T. T. (1989). *Woman, Native, Other: Writing Postcoloniality and Feminism.* Bloomington: Indiana University Press.

Minh-ha, T. T. (Director), & Bourdier, J.-P. (Co-producer). (1982). *Reassemblage: From the firelight to the screen.* Motion Picture, Senegal.

Orwell, G. (2005/1946). *Why I Write.* Harmondsworth: Penguin Books.

Paget, D. (1987). 'Verbatim Theatre': Oral History and Documentary Techniques. *New Theatre Quarterly,* 3(12), 317–336. https://doi.org/10.1017/S0266464X00002463

Polkinghorne, D. E. (1995). Narrative Configuration in Qualitative Analysis. In R. Wisniewski & J. Amos Hatch (Eds.), *Life History and Narrative* (pp. 5–23). London: Falmer Press.

Reinelt, J. (2009). Rethinking Brecht: Deconstruction, Feminism, and the Politics of Form. In M. Silberman (Ed.), *The Brecht Yearbook*. Madison: The International Brecht Society-University of Wisconsin Press.

Richardson, L. (1997). Skirting a Pleated Text: De-disciplining an Academic Life. *Qualitative Inquiry, 3*(3), 295–303. https://doi.org/10.1177/107780049700300303

Sierz, A. (2000). *In-Yer-Face Theatre: British Drama Today*. London: Faber & Faber.

Squiers, A. (2012). *The Social and Political Philosophy of Bertolt Brecht*. PhD Dissertation, Western Michigan University.

Tarker, D. (n.d.). *Towards a Feminist Theatre*. http://www.hartnell.cc.ca.us/westernstage/press_releases/2004/2005%20Info/WaitingRoomSup.htm. Accessed 6 Oct 2017.

Wake, C. (2010). Verbatim Theatre Within a Spectrum of Practices. In P. Brown (Ed.), *Verbatim: Staging Memory and Community* (pp. 6–8). Strawberry Hills: Currency Press.

Wake, C. (2013). To Witness Mimesis: The Politics, Ethics, and Aesthetics of Testimonial Theatre in Through the Wire 1. *Modern Drama, 56*(1), 102–125. https://doi.org/10.1353/mdr.2013.0009

Wang, C., & Geale, S. (2015). The power of story: Narrative inquiry as a methodology in nursing research. *International Journal of Nursing Sciences, 2*, 195–198.

CHAPTER 5

The Plays the Thing Wherein I'll Capture the Consciousness of an Audience

Abstract This chapter presents a verbatim drama script based on the stories and voices of women casual academics, unearthed through a narrative inquiry. In accordance with the advice offered by the pioneers of narrative inquiry Clandinin and Connelly, the script seeks to 'show' rather than 'tell' the findings of narrative inquiry research (Clandinin et al. 2009). The presentation of a full drama script also aligns with Hendry's (2010) and Richardson's (Qual Inq 3(3):295–303, 1997) position that qualitative and narrative research ought not to be anchored or legitimised by analysis, interpretation or verification; and responds to Cahnmann-Taylor's (2007) and Saldaña's (2010) invitation to share arts-informed research unencumbered by justification and explanation, so that others can know what it looks like (2010).

Keywords Casual academics • Drama • Narrative inquiry • Verbatim drama

In accord with the advice offered by the pioneers of narrative inquiry Clandinin and Connelly, in this chapter I seek to 'show' rather than simply 'tell' or explain the findings of a narrative inquiry research (Clandinin et al. 2009) by presenting a verbatim drama script based on the stories and voices of women casual academics. In doing so I deliberately reject the

© The Author(s) 2018
G. Crimmins, *Theatricalising Narrative Research on Women Casual Academics*, Palgrave Studies in Gender and Education, https://doi.org/10.1007/978-3-319-71562-9_5

traditional presentation of research outcomes as a non-porous cohesive account of fact; where an impenetrable band of analysis ties an 'air tight' (mono)logical argument together. Packaging 'data' which has been scraped and carved into a clear thesis positions the researcher as expert knower *on* the subject/s of the study, as the giver of knowledge, and relegates 'readers' as the unknowers.

In particular, narrative framing, through unequivocal monologic representation of data 'carvings' (or short abridged, 'samples' of data) anchored by the researcher's interpretation of the meaning it represents, restricts us from gaining our own, multiple, and diverse perspectives on research data, prevents us from acquiring individual insight, and potentially reinforces the hegemonic message that the role of the reader is to assimilate and accept the one narrative account provided. Consequently, such traditional discourse buttresses a positivist epistemology where there is one answer or truth to be gleaned from research data, and where we are expected to maintain a status of passive consumer of research; a vessel to be filled with 'knowledge'. Traditional teleological and monological narrative forms are also incongruent with the need to expand discursive forms of academic communication to accommodate feminist approaches to research, which values extra rational (Merriam et al. 2007) and multiple perspectives (Belenky et al. 1986).

Therefore, in dialectical opposition to traditional presentation of research findings I would ideally provide all the research elicited without edit, review or frame. This would afford most opportunity for multiple, diverse and individuated narrative readings and would certainly subvert the traditional role of research results/research narrative with its inherent positivist epistemology and hierarchical research relationships. Also, such full exposition of uncensored, un-ordered and un-edited 'data' narratives could express in content and form the women's narratively lived experience. Thus, an unframed and uncensored account of all the research outcomes has the most potential to present an explanation/interpretation-free polyphonic narrative account of research.

Yet, the presentation of *all* research data is both impractical and unethical. To disseminate over nine hours of interview material and tens of pages of email correspondence would be practically difficult, would preclude most research 'readers' from fully engaging in the material, and has the capacity to expose the identity of research participants (which undermines its ability to create listening ears for the yet to be voiced stories of women casual academics). And as one of the aims of creating an alternative academic discourse is to make accessible and find an audience for the lived experience of women casual academics; presenting all the data would be counter-productive. So, the unedited 'reveal' of all research data is ethically and logistically problematic.

In addition, the research data has *already* been 'carved', or at least filtered, by the epistemological, ideological and methodological choices I made in my role as researcher even before the data has been collected. Indeed, my perspectives and intentionality have already 'framed' what was selected for research in the very act of identifying a phenomenon as a curiosity, or as something worth investigating. I therefore accept that data carving and framing has already taken place in my very act of choosing an area of investigation and in adopting a narrative methodology. To some degree then, our research relationship is already separated and stratified.

But we can attempt to *limit* the power differential that currently exists between us/researcher and reader, and we can attempt to create polyphonic data narratives which have only been edited to protect the anonymity of the research participants and to make it more accessible. We can also choose to re-present research data without commentary or explanation in an invitation for readers to use their own imagination to create a personal interpretation and understanding.

So, in line with my overall aim to develop a research communication that re-presents women's lived experience of casual academia in a form that's congruent with the content, as discussed in Chaps. 3 and 4, I employed a drama/narrative structure that accommodates the unfolding, emerging and often cyclical composition of women's lived experience (Etherington 2004) and the physical, emotional and psychological, fully embodied (Merleau-Ponty 1962) nature of lived experience. I thus resituate the research outcomes of this narrative inquiry as a narrative, a story in which you can engage your imaginative and understanding self.

This decision aligns with Richardson's (1997) insight that researchers engaging in qualitative research tend to expend too much energy on their exposition of data 'analysis' in order to try to authenticate the *captured* experience and to provide evidence that they have drawn *valid* meaning. And is supported by Hendry's (2010) reflection that researchers who focus on establishing and verifying 'the truth telling of informants' within narrative research undermine their opportunity to *express* lived experience (2010, 75). Relatedly, both Hendry (2010) and Richardson (1997) suggest that qualitative and narrative research does not need to be anchored or legitimised by analysis, interpretation or verification, rather it needs to be shared. So, leaning into these ideas I present a full play script designed to

re-present or 'show' an Arts-based educational research in practice: A verbatim drama based on the lived experience of woman casual academics.
Characters:

Anna: woman in her early 30s, a married sessional academic with a PhD
Lyn: woman in her late 40s, a married sessional academic with one child
Rainee: woman in her mid-50s, a married sessional academic
Sharon: woman in her early 50s, a single parent with two children
Tasha: a Greek figure, a commentator on the action

Please note that pseudonyms are employed for people and institutions throughout the play.

Context: The current context is a university setting in 2014. Dress code, images and iconography reflect this time frame. The dress codes and iconography should locate the action in the mid-2010s to anchor the narrative historically.

PROLOGUE

Set in a lecture theatre, traditional lecture theatre lighting, lecturer/researcher (Gail) at the computer.

Gail: The research I would like to share with you today is in an arts-informed narrative inquiry into the lived experience of women casual academics.
          Arts-informed research is an approach to qualitative research in the social sciences that is informed by but not based in the arts. Its main aim is to enhance our understanding of the human condition through alternative (to conventional) representational forms of inquiry (Cole and Knowles 2008). In practice, arts-informed research merges the methodical and rigorous processes of social science inquiry with the artistic and imaginative form and qualities of the arts.
          The particular form of arts-informed inquiry that you'll see today is a verbatim drama, where the text presented employs the words and communication of research participants – verbatim. The focus of the drama is the lived experience of women casual academics.

In order to create the drama, I engaged with six women casual academics (also known as sessional staff) from across three universities in Australia and asked them an open-ended question: 'When and in what circumstance did you become a casual academic?'

END OF PROLOGUE

* * *

SCENE 1

Sharon: I'm a single mum, I came here because I fell in love with an Australian man and he wound up basically abusing me – it took me years to get out of the relationship. He strangled me, I almost died and I'm the least likely candidate for that. So I wound up learning to teach at uni to sustain my life to make me the bread winner, as a single mother...
I'm really proud of what I've done, in a foreign country. It was just so synchronistic that I was doing my Masters when they needed people to teach an undergraduate course that was linked to my study. It had me written all over it so when Steve McKeith came to town to write the course and get it organised I begged with him to tutor into it.

Anna: In 2000 I started demonstrating – and tutoring about 2002, 2003. Then in doing my PhD I picked up more tutoring. I *love* teaching, I love working with the students. It's always really rewarding to see them *get* what we're teaching, *get* the concepts we're trying to get across, to actually *see* them understand and know what to do with it is really, really rewarding. I'd always wanted to be an academic. But... this year may be my last semester, not necessarily by choice... but as a response to finances. You've got to follow the money.

Rainee: I started in 2002. I was working in a studio as a graphic designer and there was an industry association being formed. Some people from the uni came to where I was working and asked if I was interested in joining it cos I was well established in the industry. So, I was interested, yeah, I started coming to these meetings and getting to know – because the meetings took place at the uni as well – and while here I met a program director and he mentioned that he needed somebody for one of the courses he was developing. I thought yeah, I can do that 'cos almost 20 years ago I'd taught a similar course at TAFE. So, it was a natural... I was really happy to get back into teaching again.

Lyn: Twenty years ago, I was working full time as a Senior Public Servant and my daughter just got diagnosed with a brain tumour (pause). So, I just kept working, but after a year of so it just wasn't possible and I just wasn't emotionally in a... in a space where I could work full time. My daughter was nearly four at the time. So... most of that time was spent at the hospital and... and life just gets busy with appointments. And then I knew a friend who worked at the uni and she said, "Well, why don't you work as a tutor? We'd love to have somebody like you as a tutor." So, I did that and I quite enjoyed it.

Sharon: And I wasn't at the meeting but Karen told me about a meeting she was at where one of the senior people in the department said, "Oh, you know casual tutors they only do it 'cos they can't get a job anywhere else."

Anna: and I'm sure that that's a feeling amongst some, not others, but some would ask...

Rainee: "you know, why would you be a casual tutor"?

Lyn: yet there's this wealth of experience

All: we've done jobs that most academics have only read about and will never do in their whole lives.

Lyn: I was a founding member of the criminal justice commission... I used to set up new public building designs and managed huge million-dollar projects and here's some you know wanky little associate professor, specially the males, treating me like some old woman who they have to sort of 'suffer'.

Sharon: I was an established artist and art director; I lived a full and creative life I...

Rainee: I was a full time graphic designer with a large client base

Anna: and now I have my doctorate and I *always* wanted to be academic

Rainee: But I took on sessional teaching because I absolutely love teaching. I started off teaching one day a week and the rest of the time, the other four days a week I was working in the industry. It's just that I got, I got really – I really loved the teaching and there were other courses that I found that I could teach, so I wanted to apply for them.

	My kids had left home then and I didn't have – I would not have done that, taken the jump until my kids had left because of the insecurity, that's what really worried me because I had a very secure job and then to give that up.
Lyn:	So I started off with one or two core subjects, but now I teach 2nd year, 3rd year and at Masters Level and I mark Masters level papers and I do it well.
Sharon:	And I found that I absolutely loved the teaching. I'm an educator and feel strongly about the subject matter. I just was awarded an excellence in teaching award so yeah, I'm very proud of it all. I've been a sessional for 13 years and I get as many tutorials as I can and I do them well and I get enough work to create a living as a single mother.
Lyn:	And I grew to love teaching.
Anna:	I so love the teaching element of it – the interaction with the students
Lyn:	the interaction, taking a student, especially I think in a first year course because you're working so much with beginners at the learning and social level of university, working with people that you can see before your eyes transformed from scared little bunnies to people who are confident to go on – to go on...
Sharon:	to help the students find just their place, their identity and own it is really exciting.
Anna:	It's not the processes of the teaching that's the draw, for me. It's the experience of watching students find something special in whatever it is you're teaching them.
Rainee:	It's an honour being in front of the students. I bring life experience to my teaching
Lyn:	and even though sometimes you're delivering somebody else's material you're doing it through your own framework and with a creativity... to make it more interesting... and with the language and with the images that you use and the examples, they're you. They're an expression of the way that you understand and the way that you see things.
Lyn:	It's a privilege. It's amazing, I've been doing it for 20 years and I still get excited before every class
All:	every class (Lyn) every bunch of students (Lyn and Anna) every time (Lyn, Anna and Sharon) That is the real joy of it. (Lyn, Anna, Sharon and Rainee)

All: It's rewarding, you're engaged, you're excited, and you just really like the teaching.

Sharon: Oh, that shot in the arm. That rush, it's addictive. It's that engaging with the students, it's that moment when they get something or I don't know, it's fun to be the star of the show, being up front. I don't know, it's just really... So that's when I took the leap and I just quit my other job.

Lyn: It's for the students, it's not about me.

Anna: I like being at the uni. I like that student energy. I really like young people. There's that age group, that early 20s. They are just – it is the most profound time of your life. Everything is just so interesting. So, I really like being in that space.

Rainee: Most of the time it is the best job in world – and we have this opportunity to add quality to people's lives.

Lyn: And then one of the senior people in the department says, "Oh, you know casual tutors they only do it 'cos they can't get a job anywhere else."

END OF SCENE 1

***

SCENE 2

Rainee: I still enjoy the teaching, but there's this contradiction.

Anna: There's this drown or drought, the busyness and life-ness of semester and then there's this long wait in between semesters.

Sharon: I found that the worst thing about it – especially when I started doing sessional work as my main gig – was the insecurity and the gap between semesters.

Lyn: I find that wait really awful and that uncertainty, like you just don't know, you can't plan. Luckily, I had already bought a house so I didn't have to worry about... because you can't get a loan... all of those financial things are a problem.

Anna: I don't know what's happening; I don't know what's going to happen. I don't know what's going to happen... and it's almost three months or two and a half months.

Rainee: you start, well *I* start to get a bit not actually stressed but I suppose it *is* stressed, but it's something I suppose over the years I've learned to control. Because you let the stress overtake you and you can't function properly. But it's just always there in the back of your mind around where's the money coming from after this?

Lyn: You wait.

All: Life on hold.

Anna: The semester breaks, the anxiousness and frustrations... so long.

Lyn: But worrying about the future and certainty... using brain cells to worry about the future is so unproductive. It's unfair. Every time it enters my head I've had to reprogram my brain and say that university is lucky to have me. That's how I cope with the "not knowing" part of the job – those huge feelings... of uncertainty.

Sharon: I need to positive self-talk because since I suffered the domestic violence, I know I now have what is known as a victim mentality. I don't know if you know anything about the cycle of abuse in marriage but after it happens to you, you become programmed to think that it your fault that you.... get hit, that you get strangled, that you get something thrown at you. You believe you deserve it because you made it happen, so because it happened to me, I sometimes find similar thoughts going through my mind regarding sessional work... It may sound something like this: Well, I'm not really as good as the others; well it's my own fault because I didn't get that Master's degree right out of university. Or I copped out and had an arts degree instead of something that I could really use in society. So that victim mentality rears its ugly head once semester's over... And, you know, you've worked so hard and you're exhausted, so negative thoughts can settle in.

Lyn: So you'd have more security if you worked in McDonalds.

END OF SCENE 2

***

SCENE 3

Sharon: So there's this beauty and benefit in being a sessional but it comes with the uncertainty and, in my case, a knock to my self-esteem. But the biggest problem with casual work is financial.

Lyn: That's the thing... it's always... it's just always there at the forefront of your mind, always thinking about where's the money coming from? The not knowing affects your whole life. My life's on hold... and yet I've been doing this for about 20 years now.

Anna: When the car breaks down, I have to save for months before I can get it fixed. I catch buses and hang around campus for hours waiting for a bus home

Lyn: My dishwasher broke on my 50th birthday and I'm now 52 and....

Sharon: If something breaks, you don't replace it.

Rainee: We're now in a position in our fifties where we don't have enough, we can't see how we can have enough for retirement – but we've got to. My husband's got to work really, really hard and channel as much as possible into trying to recoup our losses. So, while he now has a good income... there's only a pretty modest percentage of it that can be used for living, now – living now.

Anna: and even though we may be working in a professional capacity and we're working long hours, actually the average salary is really low.

Lyn: I haven't had to pay tax for almost 20 years... Since working as a casual academic I've never earned enough to actually pay tax. And what's the tax threshold? ... about $16,000 or $18,000, but that's only in the last 12 months.

Anna: I've never earned more than $10,000 a year as a sessional, never.

Rainee: I go to an accountant at tax time because we are desperately trying to find ways to save on tax and the accountant would say, 'How do you eat?' It was a simple equation; we kept going to the bank and... extending our mortgage.

Sharon: I have a personal superannuation policy that at the moment would pay out $2500 and I'm 54. So, I've got no hope unless I get a job and work at least 15 years fulltime I'm not going to have anything other than enough super to maybe have a credit card, certainly not to be able to say that I could secure myself for retirement. And seeing emails that come around about Uni Super and stuff coming on campus to give you advice, and I think there's no point me going until I have a job.

Anna: What can they advise me to do when all I can say is 'well, in semester one I have no work'? 'I won't have an income as far as I know in semester one, unless someone asks me to tutor which I'll find out probably at the end of January'. So, I can't plan holidays, I can't plan anything.

Rainee: And that's where the guilt starts to come in where I think that's really unfair on my family and perhaps I should be looking for work outside of academia, forget about the teaching, forget about the knowledge and skills from the PhD because that's useless out in the community, nobody wants to know about that. Again, that's only useful in academia.

Sharon: And I'm always desperate for my next pay cheque, to add that to those huge feelings of uncertainty... So what happens is that I take on an enormous amount of teaching hours and it's usually anywhere... the least I teach is like 16 hours face to face... which if it was just teaching is a piece of cake, I'd love it, but it's not just teaching, it's the prepping, the marking, emailing...

Sharon: Yes, you've got to strategise. For me it's around week 10 or 11 of a semester when you get very cognisant that there's only three weeks left. I may get a couple of extra weeks' pay if I put my timesheets in at the right time – so you hold off putting in timesheets for marking and the extra OA hours and all that stuff... to stretch your income between semesters.

Rainee: I always do my taxes at the very end because you know how you get a big tax return, so that carries you through the summer, well most of it anyway, so that's my strategy. It's like a forced savings plan.

Rainee: The thing I do like strategically is I try to teach as many courses as possible because that first tutorial is worth more money. So, if I can get a few more first tutorials then I get more money, but what happens is that then I have to prepare and what I've done over the years too is I've taught, like I've tried to take on one new course every semester.

Lyn: Well, usually I try to work it out so that I'm at uni four days a week. So that way I have at least one marking day. Sometimes it works out that I'm there three days a week. Last semester, first semester, I had three days a week, but two of those days, one was a 12-hour day and one was a 13-hour day. So, it was – and you have those breaks in between, but you are there the whole –

	but it worked out because then I had days on either side, Monday and Friday to do all the prep and all of that stuff and I could do it in a more calm way.
Rainee:	But then there's the marking. A lot of marking comes in at the same time and there are these periods of intensity then...
Sharon:	week five's very intensive, that's a really intense time. And around week eight and nine that's when they all come in again. So, during the semester I work seven days a week always, like the entire semester there's never – I schedule myself so that I work early in the morning.
Sharon:	So I will get up anywhere from 3:30 and then I will work for a few hours and then take a break for breakfast. So, I have a good work schedule... it's almost like having two days in one.
Lyn:	And I work weekends as well – Oh yeah, you have to. You don't ever take a day off during the semester.
Rainee:	And even though I'm putting in all these hours there's a lot of guilt around the fact that I don't contribute enough at home... financially
Sharon:	this might sound silly – I almost see what I do as a form of community service and all of my adult life, until I was in the second year of my undergraduate degree, I would have done 10–15 hours a week of community service of one kind or I had to stop that if I was going to actually finish my degree. Now out the other end and being the teacher, I feel like I've regained that commitment that I've made as teenager to give to my community. While it's not obvious to others, because I get a pay-packet – I tracked my semester, my hours last semester, and I got paid for – what did I get, nine hours a week. There was not a week during the semester that I did less than 50 hours; that was the minimum.
Lyn:	I do lots and lots of one-on-one with students who were absolutely struggling with an advanced course they shouldn't have been enrolled into... But we all know that there's a focus on making profit, and that comes first, and students are allowed to enrol into some courses when we know they're not prepared. We know that they haven't done courses that should be prerequisites. That puts an extra burden on us.... as a sessional you've got to figure it out alone how can I not let these students that are struggling fall victim to a system that's let them come into this course that they are not prepared for.

Rainee: I get up – my alarm goes off at quarter past four in the morn-
          ing... because my husband works away. His alarm goes off at
          quarter past four so I stay in sync with him. I like to be part of
          his day. I get up then and the first thing I do after a cup of tea
          is turn on the computer and spend an hour or so replying to
          all of the emails from students overnight, I spend at least an
          hour doing emails. Then I spend time looking at the course
          material and...

Anna: I don't get enough work during the year to justify staying here.
          This year I've got two hours a week in semester one and five
          hours a week in semester two. That's not substantial enough
          pay to justify staying. Thank god my husband works. If he
          wasn't working this wouldn't be an option. We've had certainly
          moments where we've thought we can't do this, because even
          when my partner works, until this year his work wasn't sustain-
          ing us. We are borrowing money and going backwards. We now
          have a mortgage double what we had when I started my PhD...
          and that was in 2007
          That and recoup some of that debt and make the shortfall he
          now works out west and I see him once a month. So, it does, it
          affects your whole....

All: it affects your whole...life.

Anna: Life on hold.

End of Scene 3

* * *

Scene 4

Anna: This is what I would do because I always wanted to ensure
          that – because of the whole insecurity thing – that I would
          make an appointment to see the head of school, just to see – is
          there anything coming up? Am I doing the right thing? Is there
          anything where I could be doing better that would get me
          more of a permanent job or contract or whatever? I did this
          every year, every year.
          So, I would make an appointment with him and then it would
          get closer, and it would be like three weeks in advance because

he couldn't see me before that. So, then you get close to the appointment... and then it would be always cancelled or rescheduled. So, you would get the feeling like oh yeah something else has come up. I've been kind of ... replaced. Like I wasn't important enough because it's just a waste of his time. I did this every year, every year.

Rainee: Well you know you're on the outside – to the point, the fulltime academic staff were having a Christmas get together where they'd brought in things for lunch and that. One of the secretaries said, 'oh come in. There's nobody here, come in and join us'. I went in and it was like freeze. It was like 'excuse me, you're a sessional', nobody said it, but it was so obvious. It was just awful. I didn't limp from the room. I just looked at them and thought...

Sharon: And I'd been working with this sessional for about 5 or 6 years, we taught together into the same unit. And then one year she didn't come back. And I thought, 'I wonder where Kerry is', so I asked the unit coordinator and she said, 'Oh, she died. She had breast cancer and she died.' And nobody thought to tell me.

Sharon: But I don't think we're deliberately left out, I think we're just forgotten about.

END OF SCENE 4

***

SCENE 5

Lyn: It's a bit like being in a hospital, you know. I became very aware when I was in hospital with Sarah – because you're there a lot in a cancer ward. You don't complain a lot, because you're just that little bit frightened that the staff may treat you and your child not so well. So you sort of meander through.
If anything, you're trying to please, placate and be favoured. That's probably when I started drinking a lot. It is. But a lot of systems are like that when you're essentially powerless, aren't they?

Rainee: So I'd developed some really close friendships within my area and then along comes the beginning of the semester and we're not told what hours are even available until maybe two weeks before the semester starts. And when you know it's kind of like a frantic grab I suppose

Sharon: you are in competition with these people that you are really close to.

All: And I hate it

Rainee: And it can cause some really bad feelings... but there's nothing you can do, you can't speak up

Sharon: I know it's hard on full time staff also – you know they can't always plan when they're going to work either and they've got other pressures... but as a fulltime academic you have a different position in the university in terms of being able to speak up. If you've got secure tenure then you can speak up for yourself and not be fearful that next semester there'll be no work

Rainee: That's a fear I have, I don't know if it's real but it's intimidating.

Lyn: That's a burden that we carry, if we speak up for our rights there's the fear that somebody's going to say, 'too much trouble, stop offering that person work'.

Sharon: So from a... as a woman working in sessional academia, I'm very aware that this is not a power position in any way. That my job is to not cause problems for anybody. If I'm responsible, absolutely reliable, always turn up, mark properly, teach properly, don't have student complaints, I will keep getting work – and I do.

Rainee: It was brought home to me this semester – there's a colleague that has been tutoring in two of the big core subjects with me for some years. He can be quite pedantic. He got quite pedantic with the unit coordinator, who just hasn't used him this semester. So there's no recourse for him. He can't complain. He can't talk to her. He can't – she – he's just been ... blocked out. So I'm very aware of that...So you need to be really nice... you can't have an opinion that they don't like. You have to listen attentively and engage in their opinions on things, so that you're not coming in with anything that might... you can't contradict them. So much of my security is determined by the whim of the coordinator.

Lyn: There's this sessional that I used to be very, very close to and because of this thing that happened, it's hard to explain without going into detail, but there was a rift caused between us because of this course coordinator and it blew our relationship. Basically, if I was seen talking to her, like this other sessional who I used to be really close to... I would be sabotaging my job had I continued my relationship with her, which... I felt terrible. I've never gotten over it, and neither has she... how hurtful is that, that I would choose my job over a friendship?

Lyn: I don't know... it's such an energy drain and it's... frightening. Often, it's very frightening.

Anna: The middle of last year I was talking to another academic in the discipline – and I'm quite close to this person as I'd tutored with him before – and he said to me that the discipline leader told him that I was off limits... They weren't going to be giving me the teaching hours. I was off limits. Why I was off limits I don't know... so there are these silent conversations that tutors are not part of, just directly impacted by. I was shocked.

END OF SCENE 5

***

EPILOGUE

Anna: This is the complex part of being sessional... even though you feel, and you do know, we're not simple people... we're well-educated people; we know we're being exploited. We know we're ignored or forgotten about. Yet I've always said I feel like it's a privilege every time I walk on to the campus that I'm allowed to be here, and that's a real contradiction. That confuses me.

Sharon: There's always a feeling of insecurity, that doesn't go away but mostly the benefits, the joys of teaching outweigh that and buoy you on to keep going.

Lyn: So I'd be sitting up in the hospital marking papers. It was a very good thing for me to do because it was pleasurable. It sort of stretched me a bit and I could fit it in. I could still be there for my son.
And then Sarah died when she was a week off turning 12, and I did a few other things. I tried to go back to work fulltime and I joined a consulting firm and earned very good money. But I didn't really like it and I liked teaching – so came back to it.

Sharon: When I first started as sessional work in 2002 I had a different relationship with it... I was more optimistic about it.

Rainee: I had a great career path ahead of me. Over 20 years ago I was well paid. I had a full time salaried position, yeah, highly respected. I do feel that I was misled because I was – coaxed into – I was sort of courted into the idea of doing an honours degree and going on to do a Masters or a PhD in the really true belief that there was going to be a position at the end of it, that there was a growing need for people in that area, and that's not true. I now know that wasn't true.

Sharon: But there's always that possibility that it could happen, but it just hasn't for me – and I've been here for 13 years.

END OF EPILOGUE

REFERENCES

Belenky, M. F., Clinchy, B. M., Goldberger, N. R., & Tarule, J. M. (1986). *Women's Ways of Knowing: The Development of Self, Voice and Mind.* New York: Basic Books.

Cahnmann-Taylor, M. (2007). Arts-based approaches to inquiry in language education. In K. King (Ed.), *Encyclopedia of language education.* Dordrecht: Kluwer.

Clandinin, D. J., Murphy, M. S., Huber, J., & Murray-Orr, A. (2009). Negotiating narrative inquiries: Living in a tension-filled midst. *Journal of Educational Research, 103*(2), 81–90. https://doi.org/10.1080/00220670903323404

Cole, A. L., & Knowles, G. J. (2008). Arts-Informed Research. In G. J. Knowles & A. L. Cole (Eds.), *Handbook of the Arts in Qualitative Research. Perspectives, Methodologies, Examples and Issues* (pp. 55–70). Los Angeles: Sage.

Etherington, K. (2004). *Becoming a Reflexive Researcher: Using Our Selves in Research.* London: Jessica Kingsley Publishers.

Hendry, P. M. (2010). Narrative as inquiry. *The Journal of Educational Research, 103*(2), 72–80. https://doi.org/10.1080/00220670903323354

Merleau-Ponty, M. (1962). *Phenomenology of Perception.* London: Routledge.

Merriam, S. B., Caffarella, R. S., & Baumgartner, L. M. (2007). *Learning in Adulthood: A Comprehensive Guide* (3rd ed.). San Francisco: Jossey-Bass.

Richardson, L. (1997). Skirting a Pleated Text: De-disciplining an Academic Life. *Qualitative Inquiry, 3*(3), 295–303. https://doi.org/10.1177/107780049700300303

Saldaña, J. (2010). *The coding manual for qualitative researchers* (3rd ed.). London: Sage.

CHAPTER 6

A Personal Process of Restorying Lived Experience into a Proto-Verbatim Performance

Abstract This chapter discusses specific dramaturgical and theatrical decisions made to transform a proto-verbatim drama based on the lived experience of women casual academics into a piece of theatre. It particularly focuses on how the venue, staging, costuming, visual and sound effects, and direction, were designed to 'make the everyday strange' (Waters, Int Rev. Philos 30(2):137, 2011) or to startle the audience out of complacency and comfort.

YouTube videos and photographs of a performance are employed throughout the chapter to demonstrate the artistic characteristics of proto-verbatim theatre; evoke a fully embodied response; and demonstrate that 'if the research is important enough to engage the audience it will justify the time making the piece effective theatre as well as good research' (Anderson, NJ Drama Aust J 31(1):79–91, 2007, p. 87).

Keywords Arts-informed research • Casual academics • Verbatim theatre

As illustrated in the previous chapter, to fulfil my wish to re-present the words and worlds of women casual academics and to aesthetically engage an audience in stories of the 'yet to be voiced' (Arnot and Reay 2007) I developed a verbatim drama script as a research communication. Within the script I employed aspects of *écriture féminine* in order to reflect a

© The Author(s) 2018
G. Crimmins, *Theatricalising Narrative Research on Women Casual Academics*, Palgrave Studies in Gender and Education,
https://doi.org/10.1007/978-3-319-71562-9_6

woman's way of knowing and communicating (Cixous & Clement 1986; Cixous 1998) and to reflect the form of the women participants' original (story) telling. Further, as I reflected in Chap. 4, because stories shared with us/researchers reverberate *through* and *in* us as matter, and the story we re-tell in response is one that 'matters' to us, I decided upon a highly theatricalised form of verbatim drama to make manifest the 'constructed-ness' of my re-telling of the stories that had been shared with me. In this chapter, I describe how and why I transformed a drama script based on the lived experience of women casual academics into proto-verbatim theatre.

Before I do so, I briefly draw a distinction between drama and theatre, and offer a rationale for working with actors to co-creating live performance. As Fortier suggests, unlike drama, theatre is not created by words on a page, 'theatre is performance… and entails not only words but space, actors, audience and the complex relations among these elements' (Fortier 2002, 4–5), and the creation of theatre, as opposed to writing a drama, is a dynamic and collaborative process of re-translation that requires a 'letting' go of any control that you as researcher/dramatist feel you may have had over the narrative communication. It requires accepting that the actor/s with whom you work will transform the script into an embodied performance. So, the process of re-presenting Others' stories into a drama that is performed by 'other' actors (other here signifying that the actors are other than the participants) introduces an extra layer of ethical and political complexity. That is, whilst Dening suggests that a dramatist's interpretation is a transformation of the Other, and that the transformational nature of re-presentations should be made manifest (Dening 1996), the collaborative nature of creating performance (Stetson 2001; Wilkinson 2015) also requires the scholartist (Neilsen 2002), or the scholar-artist or artist- scholar, to consider the role of the actor in transforming the scripted character into a performed Other. Together, we (actors and scholartist) must take care to preserve the rhythm and intention of the original stories, whilst compelling an audience to fully listen to the Other in the story presented.

In order to achieve authenticity and audience engagement I chose to work with compassionate, skilled, and intelligent women actors, all of whom I had either worked with before, or had seen perform. I chose not to perform in the drama myself, even though I'm a trained actor, as I wanted to stand outside of the performance to assess (as objectively as im/possible) if the stories the women had shared with me could be clearly heard and seen on stage. Neither did the women casual academics who shared their stories with me perform in the drama, opting to remain anonymous. I trusted therefore that the actors would inevitably leave their mark on the performed drama and that my role (as restoryer and director) was to help shape dramatic elements into a compelling narrative.

After the initial emotional wrench of editing down the original data narrative to a play-text, the second stage of passing it on to actors to translate the script into performance was relatively easy. Working with a cast of trusted and experienced women actors, two of whom I had worked with before, and two new professional actors, one of whom serendipitously who had worked as a casual academic for many years, provided me with the confidence to pass the stories over feeling that they were in safe hands. My absolute confidence in the integrity, compassion and skill of these women (Sharon Grimley, Anna MacMahon, Rainee Skinner, Lyn Stevenson, and Natasha Tidey) ensured that the final transition of 'letting go' of my translation of the participants' stories was as easy as possible (Connelly and Clandinin 2000, 81).

Theatricalising Restoryed Data into a Proto-Verbatim Performance

In the *theatricalising* process, I used conventions from Brechtian, feminist and women's theatre, as they are designed to both aesthetically and cognitively engage an audience pieces of theatre. I specifically explain the dramaturgical decisions I made in an attempt to estrange the audience from the action, and to encourage them to see the stories of women casual academics as something of a curiosity – not inevitable or 'natural' in any way. I aimed therefore to create theatre that encourages the audience to maintain a critical lens whilst engaging with the *reconstruction* of Others' lived experience so that they could consider the social and political structures within which the women casual academic experience lay.

As discussed in Chap. 4, I decided upon the use of proto-verbatim theatre (to re-present the lived experience of women casual academics) which juxtaposes highly theatricalised presentational performance aesthetic with an emphasis on stylisation with representational performance conventions associated with naturalism. Proto verbatim corresponds to the idea that political theatre need not be devoid of theatricality, emotional or aesthetic appeal in order to fulfil the considerable potential that arts-informed research has to powerfully connect with audiences (Anderson 2007). It also practically applies the idea that arts-informed research 'must take account of the aesthetic demands of theatre' if it is to create social change (Anderson 2007, 89). Indeed, Thompson's (2009) considers that there has been a significant shift in political and applied theatre practice from the 'effective to the affective' and as mentioned, that theatre that is 'affective' has a longer lasting impact on audiences (Thompson 2009). So, in the discussion below I also explicate how I, along with the creativity of a talented cast, designed a proto-verbatim performance to ethically, cognitively and emotionally engage an audience in the lived experience of women casual academics.

I embed into the discussion photographs and YouTube videos of the performance as visual and aural illustrations of the theatre event in response to Saldaña's request that arts-informed researchers offer detailed documentation of their/our work to inform the readership of what this genre looks like (2010). I also use images of the event to support Langer's (1942, 1962) insight that images are a primordial form of communication and way of knowing, and demonstrate how research can 'move off the shelves' (Lenfant 2003, 869).

The Theatre Event

I chose to present the live performance of the proto-verbatim drama based on the lived experience of women casual academics within university research conferences – environments populated with casual academics, academics with ongoing employment, heads of university schools and faculties, and university senior management; an audience Denzin identifies as a professional gathering of scholars (1997). My decision to present the drama in a public context for the was informed by Rindfleish et al.'s (2009) position that the-presentation of women academics' stories in public places can be used to resist the hegemony of privileged stories of academia, and that more stories need to be heard in openly public spaces that recognise the ongoing disadvantage women experience in academics. In addition, the public context was chosen to allow the stories of women causal academics to become publicly known and to counter the dominant organisational stories of academia (Boje 1995). It also allowed for the dominant and official narratives that universities present, via internal and external public communications, can be brought into dialectical relationship with the lived experience of the women casual academics, and for these women to have an opportunity for their story to be heard (Boje 1995). Further, the choice of context aligned with Valentine's (n.d.)

suggestion that bringing communities of interest into the theatre allows participants/contributors 'that essential human right of being able to see themselves and their community conjured to the stage and thereby reflect on both the strengths and injustices of your world', to 'give back' to the community from which they have drawn stories, and 'to become in a very real way a continuing part of the life and narrative of the community represented' (Valentine n.d.).

HOW THE MISE-EN-SCÈNE SOUGHT TO MAKE STRANGE THE EVERYDAY

My challenge was to make strange the familiar, to reframe as curious the everyday, or to reposition the seemingly natural and universal as a thing to be studied and understood. I wanted for the audience to see anew the lives of women casual academics, so I created a theatrical chorus. Not a chorus as in a chorus line, or a choir, but a chorus as used in Greek drama, a collective of individuals who stand slightly outside of the main action and peer into it, offering social critique and commentary, chanting the seeming wrongs of systems of power. The central actors of the drama, representing the women casual academics, moved in and out of the chorus to provide monologue, dialogue, before returning to offering critical commentary. This anti-naturalistic use of a chorus also afforded me the opportunity to create a multiplicity of characters in a multi-vocal drama in order to subvert 'the dominant hegemony of univocal forms of patriarchal theatre' (Lyons and Lyons 1994, 57) where one male central character moves from conflict to resolution and salvation. I also positioned four actors side by side centre stage to tell the stories of six women casual academics, and to comment on each other's stories, so that no one character was de/privileged. The following photograph (Fig. 6.1 Every woman has a story) illustrates the equal positioning and privilege each character and chorus member was afforded in the scripting and direction.

I employed costuming to create the current historical epoch; the context in which the original stories were shared. This aligned with Laughlin's position that costuming in political theatre should be historically representative and 'not fixed and universally human' (Laughlin 1990, 152), which could point to an inevitability of circumstance. Additionally, each woman wore a red silk scarf to both represent a unification between the women characters and highlight the staged or constructed nature of the re-presentation. The scarves were also used to symbolise how senior academics' demeaning views

Fig. 6.1   Every woman has a story

of casual academics can cause women to feel 'gagged' by senior academics. So, on the line, 'oh you know sessional staff, they only do it because they can't get a job doing anything else', the actors used their scarves to externalise the internal pain inflicted by demeaning and disparaging comments. In particular, the scarves were used to strangle, gag, choke and stab at the women. This is illustrated in the following image (Fig. 6.2):

Finally, the scarves also became blindfolds to communicate how short-term teaching contracts made it difficult for women casual academics to plan or even visualise/see the future (Fig. 6.3).

Along with the re-presentational and historicising costuming I employed stark and representational staging, assisted by the use of direct audience address with which the actor presented their character's stories of academia. Stark lighting and direct address were used to reinforce the 'staged' nature of the theatre event (Richardson 2007) and to support a defamiliarisation or strange making process. As Chiari suggests, 'the alien-ation device presents the familiar world in an estranging or defamiliarizing manner to make the audience see the things which they have not noticed beforehand. It prevents the audience from evaluating things in a habitual manner by opening a fresh perspective' (Chiari 1971, 164). Presenting the

Fig. 6.2 They only do it because they can't get a job doing anything else

Fig. 6.3 I can't plan

stories with deliberate staging is akin to putting a frame around the action, inviting an audience to look closely inside the frame and consider its features.

Therefore, these general elements of the *mise-en-scène*, such as the venue and context, lighting and costuming were used in an attempt to make strange the lived experience of women casual academics. I next discuss one or two key dramaturgical elements employed within each scene, accompanied by photographs and YouTube videos, in order to address Cahnmann-Taylor's (2007) and Saldaña's (2010) requests to see examples of what arts-informed research actually looks and sounds like.

PROLOGUE: AN ARTS-INFORMED NARRATIVE INQUIRY

I introduced the proto-verbatim theatre performance with a prologue to explicitly demonstrate the staged re-presentational nature of the research. I stood behind a lectern and discussed the basic aims and practices of arts-informed narrative inquiry to contextualise the drama the audience was about to 'witness' (Phelan 2004). I used the five-minute introduction as a meta-theatrical gesture employed to 'foreground the drama's construction process' in a similar fashion to the actors' introduction in The Paper Birds' proto-verbatim theatre production of *Others* (Duggan 2013). Whilst I verbally addressed the audience, as if in a traditional research presentation, I projected the title of the scene in large white letters on a black background onto the back wall of the stage to introduce both the episodic structure of the play and illuminate the main idea explored in the scene. Projecting scene titles onto the stage is a Brechtian convention that many feminist theatre companies employ to dissipate emotional identification and suspense (Laughlin 1990). They act also as a comment on the action in the foreground.

SCENE 1: WHEN AND IN WHAT CIRCUMSTANCE DID YOU BECOME A CASUAL ACADEMIC?

The first scene opened with a harsh white spotlight on the first speaker's face and torso. There was no attempt made to conceal the mechanics of the lights as the lighting operator and floor spots were placed in full view of the audience to focus the audience's attention on the theatrical construction of the performance. As each actor began to talk to the audience so a light would be shone on that actor. As I mentioned earlier the women/actors/chorus delivered juxtaposing monologues, dialogue and commentary to the audience in an attempt to create 'multiple mutually authorising voices' where no one dominant protagonist or narrative was privileged (Claycomb 2003, 97). I employed this technique to correspond with the techniques and aims of feminist and political theatre where an interruption to the hierarchy of a coherent, explanatory narrative is designed to support democratising power. The device allowed me 'to reveal a hidden truth, to give voice to silenced voices, or to explore what has been kept hidden' (Claycomb 2003, 99). A more detailed illustration is presented can be found at https://www.youtube.com/watch?v=kHit41xcFRE

Scene 2: And Then There's This Long Wait in Between Semesters

Throughout Scene 2 the back wall wore a projected image of the four women actors sat on black seats wearing red scarves as blindfolds to convey the long wait women casual academics endure between semesters, and to express their inability to plan or see a future. The image was therefore presented to reinforce the *gestus* of the scene or the physical representation of social gestus of social injustice (Reinelt 2009).

In addition to the image of women wearing scarves as blindfolds, the delivery of the women's short monologues and dialogues were interrupted with the sound effect of a train approaching. This theatrical metaphor re-established the constructed nature of the re-presentation and developed the women's narrative. In response to the sound the women stood, hopefully and expectantly, only to hear it pass without stopping. The train was symbolic of ongoing employment opportunities and the passing train symbolised the passing hope. Also in this scene I introduced a singer, again resonant of a Greek theatre choral figure, to comment on the action, heighten the theatricality of the performance, and aesthetically engage the audience. The actor representing the singer sang with beauty and significant skill to both exteriorise the women characters self-talk and emotion, and to captivate and engage the audience aesthetically. You can view the scene at https://www.youtube.com/watch?v=46UySViATSg

SCENE 3: BUT THE BIGGEST PROBLEM WITH CASUAL WORK IS FINANCIAL

The title of Scene 3 was taken from a line in an interview which seemed to encapsulate a sentiment shared by all the women casual academics with whom I engaged. For this scene, I created a visual metaphor for the many unpaid hours that women casual academics' work (preparing for teaching, marking and answering email) as similar to unpaid domestic work. The metaphor became the scene's gestus. As the actors directly delivered their lines to the audience they continuously and frantically put washing on and off a clothes line held by a Greek chorus figure and one of the other actors. Following the advice of theatre artist, and casual academic Guillermo Verdecchia, theatre artists have a *responsibility to the truth*, '*but not necessarily to the literal, surface details of the truth*' (Verdecchia 2006, 335). Truth, as Verdecchia understands it, does not attempt to present an illusion of reality through mimetism; rather truth is found in the absence of mimetism through a heightened theatricalised experience (Verdecchia 2006). The following image illustrates the theatricalised essence of the women's relentless and under/unpaid work experience (Fig. 6.4):

Fig. 6.4   A relentless and underpaid work experience

The use of a visual metaphor also reflected the feminine imagistic way of knowing to represent our understanding of the main idea within each scene (Fleckenstein 1996; Langer 1942, 1962), and highlighted the constructedness of research re-presentation. Indeed, Dening (1996) notes that rather than mimetically representing any Other in verbatim drama, an arts-informed dramatist should make explicit their interpreted nature of the Other's experience. I therefore re-presented the experience of women casual academics through visual metaphor to make explicit the constructed and interpreted nature of my re-presentation. You can view Scene 3 at https://www.youtube.com/watch?v=UIlwif-cNsI

SCENE 4: JILTED

I presented the title for Scene 4 on a large screen behind the action to introduce the central motif/idea of the scene – that women casual academics feel on the periphery of university life, ignored, jilted, and left waiting. The metaphor illuminates the action where an actor tells of how she has arranged to meet her Head of School "just to see… is there anything that would get me more of a permanent job or contract or whatever?" whilst the other actors dress her in a wedding dress, veil and pass her flowers. In doing so the meeting is presented as analogous to a bride meeting her groom; as the bride prepares with expectation and hope, to meet a man that may offer security and commitment.

However, as the actor/character tells the audience that the meeting with her Head of School is cancelled, or postponed, "every year… every year" she becomes sad and life-less. In order to reinforce the loss of optimism the backdrop transitions from the first image (Fig. 6.5: Hopeful) to a second image (Fig. 6.6 Jilted).

I use photographs to heighten the feelings of loss and dejection the woman casual academic seems to experience at having the meeting cancelled, and to theatricalise 'the essence' of the scene (Wake 2013). I specifically employed visual elements as Barone and Eisner (1997) suggest that they 'make it possible to formulate meanings that elude linguistic description '(Barone and Eisner 1997, 90). In addition, the images employed helped to imagistically communicate the narrative in a feminine form of knowing and communicating (Fleckenstein 1996; Langer 1942, 1962). Please view the scene at https://www.youtube.com/watch?v=PBrIndD4Uus

Fig. 6.5   Hopeful

Fig. 6.6   Jilted

SCENE 5: THERE'S NOTHING YOU CAN DO, YOU CAN'T SPEAK UP

I also exploited the aesthetic power of photographs to express the women casual academics' lack of voice within the university within Scene 5. Throughout most of the scene one choral figure/character stands motionless with her hands covering her mouth, representing sense of voicelessness. See Fig. 6.7, 'You can't speak up', was thus presented as the gestus and backdrop to the stage action.

I introduced images and non-naturalistic elements to also invite the audience to look at the dramatic action with a critical lens, or with estranged eyes (Chiari 1971, 164; Squiers 2012). Finally, I directed the scene so that the character featured above lets out a loudly and unexpected scream (Fig. 6.8).

The pitch and volume of the scream were much higher and louder than the rest of the oral delivery so the highly theatricalised moment of action was designed to shock the audience out of any sense of complacency or comfort and to 'make the performance memorable… through

Fig. 6.7 You can't speak up

Fig. 6.8 Often it's very frightening

moments of dramatic and theatrical awe' (Saldaña 2011, 122). There were several moments of theatrical surprise designed to re-awaken the audience from a comfortable rhythm of narrative. The action is best illustrated in the following YouTube video: https://www.youtube.com/watch?v=kNWzLxGZrGE

Epilogue **This is the complex part of being sessional... we're not simple people... we're well-educated people.**

Despite the focus on the anti-naturalistic performance aesthetic I discuss above, many aspects of the performances were also designed to develop empathetic characterisation and the arousal of empathy in the audience, as 'performed data has an empathetic power and dimension often lacking in standard qualitative research narratives' (Mienczakowski et al. 2002, 34). Furthermore, for Eisner (2008) empathetic character representation and performance requires artistry in research that 'puts a premium on evocation' (Eisner 2008, 91). I therefore directed the women to reveal their felt emotion through their paralinguistics, facial expression, posture and gesture. In particular, I directed the actor show so that the line, "When I first started as sessional work in 2002 I had a different relationship with it... I was more optimistic about it", was delivered with vocal and facial expressions of sadness and deep regret. I thus wanted the audience to engage both empathetically *and* critically with the stories of women casual academics, to be both engaged in and estranged by the action, song and images of proto-verbatim theatre. The directorial decisions are illustrated in the following YouTube video: https://www.youtube.com/watch?v=HxO0PRz8cOI

Use of Metaphor

In his treatise on rhetoric Aristotle claimed that metaphors consist in giving a thing a name that belongs to something else. Like allegories and similes, metaphors draw attention to similarities between two seemingly disparate phenomena, and as such are a useful tool for drawing parallels, and for seeing things we may have otherwise missed (Schon 1993). Metaphors also surface the taken-for-granted assumption of the person/s using the metaphor (Lyddon et al. 2001), and can be used to lead to new insights (Schon 1993). Finally, they employ a highly economical language to describe unseen though pertinent relations.

For these reasons, I employed several metaphors in the proto-verbatim theatre piece on the lived experience of women casual academics. For instance, I used blindfolds to allude to the women's lack of ability to see or plan the future, a train passing was employed to suggest the women's wait for ongoing work opportunities (that never seem to eventuate); I employed being left at the altar to resemble the women casual academics' expressed feelings of abandonment; and non-stop domestic duties were used to index the relationship between relentless, unpaid, and often unrecognised 'housework' within the home and academia. Thus, metaphors – communicated through costume, sound effects, song and staging – did not explicitly make manifest the perceived relationship between two seemingly different phenomena; but relationship and resonances were suggested, or implied.

Indeed, I used theatrical metaphors to economically and artistically share *my* (one) understanding and reaction to the women's stories, and so maintained an openness of interpretation (and imagination). I thus consciously avoided determining closed or monologic readings by merely hinting at feelings of abandonment, or relentless work or wait. This deliberate direction aligns with Sikes and Gale's (2006) suggestion that arts-based research ought to *evoke* an aesthetic and emotional response from an audience, and that evocation requires narrative space for audiences to use their imagination to construct their own ideas and emotions in a work. Likewise, Bruner (1990) suggests that narrative space or 'undetermination' requires the storyteller to leave some gaps within the narrative to allow audiences to create their own meaning, and Gerrig describes a good story as being able to transport the reader into the narrative world by providing small spaces into which the reader can 'use their own experiences of the world to bridge the gaps in the text' (1993, 17). I therefore employed theatrical metaphors in order to create space in the performance for audiences to engage in the stories using their own imaginations, emotions and logics, whilst seeking to entertain them and share my understanding (refraction) of the women's stories shared to me.

Yet, because metaphors shape the way we think and make some things salient while 'disappearing' others, the manner in which we (as schol-artists) present them is as important as the meaning of the metaphor. For instance, Saldaña suggests that the researcher has both 'an ethical obligation to recreate an authentic representation of reality' and a 'license for artistic interpretation of that reality' (2005, 32). I thus chose to use highly theatricalised metaphors in order to avoid 'thinking like a social scientist' and to shape the performances with attention to 'substance and style, form and feeling, research *and* art' (Saldaña 2011, 203). Correspondingly, Saldaña proposes that 'if art is to imitate life, then art needs to do so in an engaging manner for its audience' (2005, 204). In the development of the theatre event I therefore spent a great deal of time and creative energy to engage the audience's in the yet to be voiced (Arnot and Reay 2007) stories of women casual academics, as 'if it is important enough to engage the audience it will justify the time making the piece effective theatre as well as good research' (Anderson 2007, 87). In particular, I textured the performance space with gestus, white light, choral commentary, direct address, emotional and imaginative evocation, and theatrical metaphor, in an embodied and imagistic performance aesthetic, as I felt women casual academics deserved to have their stories presented with artistry and 'connoisseurship' (Eisner 2008). The art in art-informed research is of equal, if not more, importance than the substantive content of the research. It needs to compel an audience's attention and evoke an emotional and cognitive response. Sitting with McCall (1993) I believe that that researchers wanting to develop performed research should collaborate with theatre professionals 'who are trained in theatre and performance techniques' to provide guidance and advice on how interpretive choices are made using theatrical devices (2003, 130), as audience's expect good theatre and research participants deserve for the their stories to be (re) told well.

Closing Thoughts

In this chapter, I reflected on and illustrate some of the specific dramaturgical and theatrical decisions I made in transforming a proto-verbatim drama as a piece of theatre and discuss my role in creating a m*ise-en-scène* (including decisions pertaining to the venue, staging, costuming, visual and sound effects, and direction) through which I sought to 'make the everyday strange' (Waters 2011) to startle the audience out of complacency and comfort. I also briefly considered how metaphor can engage an audience's imagination to see similarities between two seemingly dissimilar phenomena, and that the researcher has both 'an ethical obligation to recreate an authentic representation of reality' and a 'license for artistic interpretation of that reality' (Saldaña 2005, 32). In the following chapter, I discuss how the performance was received by the research participants and audiences, and the impact it had on them, in order to (part) evaluate if and how these aims were achieved.

REFERENCES

Anderson, M. (2007). Making Theatre from Data: Lessons for Performance Ethnography from Verbatim Theatre. *NJ Drama Australia Journal*, *31*(1), 79–91. http://search.informit.com.au/fullText;res=AEIPT;dn=168557

Arnot, M., & Reay, D. (2007). A Sociology of Pedagogic Voice: Power, Inequality and Pupil Consultation. *Discourse: Studies in the Cultural Politics of Education*, *28*(3), 311–325. https://doi.org/10.1080/01596300701458814

Barone, T. E., & Eisner, E. (1997). Arts-Based Educational Research. In R. M. Jaeger (Ed.), *Complementary Methods for Research in Education* (pp. 72–116). Washington, DC: American Education Research Association.

Boje, D. M. (1995). Stories of the Storytelling Organization: A Postmodern Analysis of Disney as "Tamara-Land". *The Academy of Management Journal*, *38*(4), 997–1035. https://doi.org/10.2307/256618

Bruner, J. S. (1990). *Acts of Meaning*. Cambridge: Harvard University Press.

Cahnmann-Taylor, M. (2007). Arts-Based Approaches to Inquiry in Language Education. In K. King (Ed.), *Encyclopaedia of Language Education*. Dordrecht: Kluwer.

Chiari, J. (1971). *Landmarks of Contemporary Drama*. New York: Gordian Press.

Cixous, H. (1998). *Stigmata: Escaping Texts*. London: Routledge.

Cixous, H., & Clement, C. (1986). *The newly born woman*. Minneapolis: University of Minnesota Press.

Claycomb, R. M. (2003). (Ch) Oral History: Documentary Theatre, the Communal Subject and Progressive Politics. *Journal of Dramatic Theory and Criticism*, *2*, 95–122, https://journals.ku.edu/index.php/jdtc/article/view/3474

Connelly, F. M., & Jean Clandinin, D. (2000). *Narrative Inquiry: Experience and Story in Qualitative Research*. San Francisco: Jossey-Bass.

Dening, G. (1996). *Performances*. Chicago: University of Chicago Press.

Denzin, N. K. (1997). Performance Texts. In W. G. Tierney & Y. S. Lincoln (Eds.), *Representation and the Text: Re-framing the Narrative Voice* (pp. 179–217). Albany: State University of New York Press.

Duggan, P. (2013). Others, spectatorship, and the ethics of verbatim performance. *New Theatre Quarterly*, *29*(2), 146–158. https://doi.org/10.1017/s0266464x13000250

Eisner, E. W. (2008). Art and Knowledge. In J. Gary Knowles & A. L. Cole (Eds.), *Handbook of the Arts in Qualitative Research, Perspectives, Methodologies, Examples and Issues* (pp. 3–12). Thousand Oaks: Sage.

Fleckenstein, K. S. (1996). Images, Words, and Narrative Epistemology. *College English*, *58*(8), 914–933. http://www.jstor.org/stable/378229

Fortier, M. (2002). *Theory/Theatre: An Introduction*. London: Routledge.

Gerrig, R. J. (1993). *Experiencing Narrative Worlds: On the Psychological Activities of Reading*. New Haven: Yale University Press.

Langer, S. K. (1942). *Philosophy in a New Key*. Cambridge: Harvard University Press.

Langer, S. K. (1962). *Philosophical Sketches*. Baltimore: Johns Hopkins University Press.

Laughlin, K. (1990). Brechtian Theory and American Feminist Theatre. In P. Kleber & C. Visser (Eds.), *Reinterpreting Brecht: His Influence on Contemporary Drama and Film* (pp. 147–160). Cambridge: Cambridge University Press.

Lenfant, C. (2003). Clinical Research to Clinical Practice – Lost in Translation? *The New England Journal of Medicine, 349*(9), 868–874. https://doi.org/10.1056/NEJMsa035507

Lyddon, W. J., Clay, A. L., & Sparks, C. L. (2001). Metaphor and Change in Counseling. *Journal of Counseling and Development, 79*(3), 269–274. https://doi.org/10.1002/j.1556-6676.2001.tb01971.x

Lyons, C., & Lyons, J. (1994). Anna Deveare Smith: Perspectives on Her Performance Within the Context of Critical Theory. *Journal of Dramatic Theory and Criticism, 9*(1), 43–65. https://journals.ku.edu/index.php/jdtc/issue/archive

McCall, M. M. (1993). *Not 'Just' a Farmer and Not Just a 'Farm Wife'*. Unpublished Performance Script.

Mienczakowski, J., Smith, L., & Morgan, S. (2002). Seeing Words – Hearing Feelings: Ethnodrama and the Performance of Data. In C. Bagley & M. B. Cancienne (Eds.), *Dancing the Data* (pp. 34–52). New York: Peter Lang.

Neilsen, L. (2002). Learning from the Liminal: Fiction as Knowledge. *Alberta Journal of Education Research, 48*(3), 206–214. http://ajer.journalhosting.ucalgary.ca/index.php/ajer/article/viewFile/326/318. Accessed 28 Sept 2017.

Phelan, P. (2004). Marina Abramović: Witnessing Shadows. *Theatre Journal, 56*(4), 569–577. https://doi.org/10.2307/25069529

Reinelt, J. (2009). Rethinking Brecht: Deconstruction, Feminism, and the Politics of Form. In M. Silberman (Ed.), *The Brecht Yearbook*. Madison: The International Brecht Society-University of Wisconsin Press.

Richardson, L. (2007). Writing: A method of inquiry. In N. K. Denzin & Y. S. Lincoln (Eds.), *Handbook of qualitative research* (2nd ed., pp. 923–948). Thousand Oaks: Sage Publications.

Rindfleish, J., Sheridan, A., & Kjeldal, S.-E. (2009). Creating an "Agora" for Storytelling as a Way of Challenging the Gendered Structures of Academia. *Equal Opportunities International, 28*(6), 486–499. https://doi.org/doi:10.1108/02610150910980783

Saldaña, J. (2005). *Ethnodrama: An Anthology of Reality Theatre (Crossroads in Qualitative Inquiry Series)*. Walnut Creek: AltaMira Press.

Saldaña, J. (2010). The Backstage and Offstage Stories of Ethnodrama: A Review of Ackroyd & O'toole's Performing Research. *International Journal of Education & the Arts, 1*(Review 5). http://www.ijea.org/v11r5/

Saldaña, J. (2011). *Ethnotheatre: Research from Page to Stage* (Vol. 3). Walnut Creek: Left Coast Press.

Schön, D. A. (1993). Generative Metaphor: A Perspective on Problem-Setting in Social Policy. In A. Ortony (Ed.), *Metaphor and Thought* (pp. 135–161). Cambridge: Cambridge University Press.

Sikes, P., & Gale, K. (2006). *Narrative Approaches to Education Research.* Plymouth: Faculty of Education, University of Plymouth.

Squiers, A. (2012). *The Social and Political Philosophy of Bertolt Brecht.* PhD Dissertation, Western Michigan University.

Stetson, K. (2001). Horse High, Bull Strong, Pig Tight: A Play for One Actor in Two Acts. In B. Barton (Ed.), *Marigraph: Gauging the Tides of Drama from New Brunswick, Nova Scotia, and Prince Edward Island* (pp. 395–423). Toronto: Playwrights Union of Canada.

Thompson, J. (2009). *Performance Affects: Applied Theatre and the End of Effect.* Basingstoke: Palgrave Macmillan.

Valentine, Alana. (n.d.). *The Tune of the Spoken Voice.* http://www.alanavalentine.com/media/australian-writers-guild-magazine.pdf. Accessed 6 Oct 2017.

Verdecchia, G. (2006). Blahblahblahblah Mememememe Theatreschmeatre. In S. Grace & J. Wasserman (Eds.), *Theatre and Autobiography.* Vancouver: TalonBooks.

Wake, C. (2013). To witness mimesis: The politics, ethics, and aesthetics of testimonial theatre in through the wire, modern. *Drama, 56*(1), 102–125. https://doi.org/10.1353/mdr.2013.0009

Waters, S. (2011). Political Playwriting: The Art of Thinking in Public. *An International Review of Philosophy, 30*(2), 137. https://doi.org/10.1007/s11245-011-9100-0

Wilkinson, L. (2015). Working Together: Collaborative Journeys in Cross-Cultural Research and Performance. In M. Anderson & P. O'Connor (Eds.), *Applied Theatre: Research.* London: Bloomsbury.

CHAPTER 7

A Re-view of the Process and Impact of Theatricalising Narrative Research on Women Casual Academics

Abstract This *re*-view of a research process dedicated to unearthing and theatricalising the lived experience of women casual academics 'promiscuously' (Childers et al. Int J Qual Stud Educ 26(5):507–523, 2013) breaks the cardinal rule of academic writing by introducing new ideas into the conclusion. Such stretching of academic convention allowed me to discuss the storying nature of women casual academics' communication, and accommodated research participants and audiences' reflections on the theatricalization of women casual academics' stories. These reflections captured the political potential of theatre, a cognitive, corporeal and emotional response to theatricalised research, and the capacity of arts-informed research to radically transform research data and audiences' engagement, to celebrate a multiplicity of stories, storytellers, and story *forms* through which we can communicate research stories.

Keywords Arts-informed research • Casual academics • Storying • Feminist research

This final chapter offers a re-view of a research process of unearthing and theatricalising the lived experience of women casual academics. In keeping with a central preoccupation within this book, I propose that 'new bottles for new wine' are required, or that new forms through which to

© The Author(s) 2018
G. Crimmins, *Theatricalising Narrative Research on Women Casual Academics*, Palgrave Studies in Gender and Education,
https://doi.org/10.1007/978-3-319-71562-9_7

communicate education research are required to accommodate new content. In alignment with this notion I do not offer any neat conclusions to this book. Instead, because new forms and structures reflect a growth or blossoming I predominantly re-view ideas and practices that either continue to puzzle or excite me, ideas or reflections that compels me to (Fig. 7.1)

read more,
think more,
and engage more in this area of research.

I therefore 'promiscuously' (Childers et al. 2013) break the cardinal rule of academic writing by introducing some new ideas or reflections into this chapter. The conscious break with tradition reflects an alignment with this work and 'in-the-making' (Childers et al. 2013), emerging processes and communications of feminist research, and allows for some of the research participants' and audience's reflections on a verbatim performance (based on their lived experience) to be re-presented.

Fig. 7.1 Theatricalising narrative research on women casual academics

I introduce what I understand, at this point in time, about engaging in an art- informed narrative inquiry into the lived experience of women casual academics by sharing two short stories. I encapsulate my understanding in stories as the entire book is predicated on the notion that we both come to know, and share what our understanding, through storytelling and narrative. As Clandinin and Connelly (2000) presented, people lead storied lives and tell stories of those lives.

> The author and critic Alberto Manguel (1997) embarked on a project about the history of reading. After writing several essays, he asked himself, 'What could bring all these bits of lore, however rich and quaint, into any but the most arbitrary coexistence?' And suddenly it struck me: I was the cognitive link... I soon understood that the I working through the text was not I, Alberto Manguel, but the author who had collected his wares for public display and was now arguing their worth and relevance. Strictly from the point of view of craft, what mattered was that the I on the page gave the reader a place from which to start, or a chair in which to sit, or (to change metaphors) the I played a B flat to which the readers could tune their instruments.... Brazenly idiosyncratic, I freed the book to be A History of Reading, not The History of Reading (Manguel 1997 as cited in Neilsen 2002, 16).

Neilsen shared Manguel's story in order to reflect a philosophical shift from knowledge to know*ing*. That is, a shift from *The* to *A,* from presenting The Answer and The Way, to being open to and sharing many possible answers (Neilsen 2002). Manguel's story reflects a postmodern sensibility within which there are no single answers and firm conclusions to be drawn. Instead there are juxtaposing perspectives and stories of lived experience, each worthy of consideration; each offering a reader/viewer 'a chair in which to sit' for a while.

The second short story I share is about how the Professor of Drama at the University of Exeter, Professor Chris McCullough, explained the theoretical and aesthetic development of theatre movements or genres by claiming 'new bottles are needed for new wine'. In particular, he suggested that emerging philosophical, ideological, political and social ideas require, and shape, new forms of expression, or 'new bottles for new wine'. McCullough's metaphor seems relevant to academic research too, where the form and structure of a research communication should bend, stretch or rupture in response to the shape of its content and philosophical core. Indeed, I conceptualise that new forms and structures reflect a growth or blossoming, as 'every seed destroys its container, or else there would be no fruition' (Scott-Maxwell 1979, 65).

Correspondingly, this book seeks to trouble the restrictive masculinity of linear and rational argument so It would be incongruent for me to now include a definitive or trustworthy conclusion to create an encapsulated whole (Bloomberg and Volpe 2012). Therefore, in line with Blumenreich (2004) who suggests that contemporary narratives 'resist the conventional "resolution" of standard narratives that stabilise meaning and implicitly favour a single interpretation' (2004, 79), I apply a newer/current lens to re-consider the project I describe in Chaps. 1, 2, 3, 4, 5, and 6. In doing so I point to the messy, layered and iterative nature of re-search where understanding emerges and increases through a layering of re-reading and reflection. This final chapter thus contains part-past and part-present reflection as I describe what I *did*, what I *came* to understand and what I am currently coming to know – on reviewing past ideas or practices. I shall reflect a re-view process by using both present and past tenses to illuminate my again and seeing anew what I have previously seen or done.

Therefore, in this final chapter I present my current/latest reflections on the discoveries and understandings of engaging in collating and theatricalising the stories of women casual academics in Australia. In doing so some passages of text will summarise or re-state some of the learnings or dawnings I encounter/ed through undertaking the research project, and some passages will contain new realisations or thoughts encountered during a re-view process, thus stretching and nudging open the structure/stricture of the traditional research communication.

How Women Casual Academics Shared Their Stories

When I reflect on how women casual academics describe their lived experience, I both consider the *way* the women shared their experiences, as well as *what* they shared with me. I therefore first discuss the form of their storied communication and secondly consider some of the commonly expressed experiences contained in the women's stories.

My re-view of the communications gifted to me by women illuminated that the women shared their experiences in stories, not narratives. The difference between stories and narratives as explained by Boje (2001), is that stories are a telling in the present tense and narratives are retrospective accounts of past events, coupled with explanations that bind and determine the teller's meaning of the experience/event (Boje 2001). That is, narratives are told *about* an event or experience of the past and are recounted with a clear perspective on the past. Whereas, for Boje (2001), stories possess a 'pre' or 'antenarrative' structure and tend to be non-linear and less 'plotted' than narratives. They also represent the feelings and experiences of people at their time of telling, and so fail to create a unified and cohesive form or meaning. Stories are thus usually presented in fragments, 'bits that are told here and there', as there is no 'whole' story (Boje 2001, 5). Stories or antenarratives for Boje (2001) also inhabit detail and poetic, expressive language. I understand from this that stories are 'in-the- making' (Childers et al. 2013) vivid and expressive accounts of experience *as it is lived,* and excludes a coherence that is added to a story through a post-edit, post-experience assimilation and evaluation of the experience. Looking again at the women's shared stories I noted the use of present tense, the disjointed, non-chronological tellings of events, the detail in the tellings and their lyrical and evocative turn of phrase. Examples of the women speaking of their now in the present tense include 'I love teaching, I love working with the students... ; I'm an educator and feel strongly about the subject matter; Well, why don't you work as a tutor? We'd love to have somebody like you as a tutor...; Oh, that shot in the arm. That rush, it's addictive.... '. Also, many of the women's sentences or ideas trail/ed off or are were picked up again in later com-munications, fragments 'of bits' reflective of a lack of completion and theorisation, missing a post-experience reflection. Examples include: 'I still enjoy the teaching, but there's this contradiction...; I find the wait really awful and that uncertainty, like you just don't know, you can't plan...; I don't know what's happening... I don't know what's going to happen. I don't know what's going to happen...and it's almost three months or two and a half months; The semester breaks, the anxiousness and frustrations... so long; my life's on hold... I have to save for months before I can get it fixed. I catch buses and hang around campus for hours waiting for a bus home.

The women in this study also employed poetic descriptions by using analogies and metaphors in their stories, again characteristic of storytell-ing: '... it's almost like having two days in one; There's this drown or drought, the busyness and life-ness of semester and then there's this long wait in between semesters', and detailed descriptions: 'I get up... my alarm goes off at quarter past four in the morning... because my husband works away. His alarm goes off at quarter past four so I stay in sync with him. I like to be part of his day; The middle of last year I was talking to another academic in the discipline, and I'm quite close to this person as I'd tutored with him before, and he said to me that the discipline leader told him that

I was off limits… They weren't going to be giving me the teaching hours. I was off limits; So I will get up anywhere from 3:30 and then I will work for a few hours and then take a break for breakfast….'

Through re-viewing the way in which the women participants describe/d their experience I am compelled to re-consider the narrative epistemology I employ/ed in this project. Although I still accept that we come to know and express what we know through narrative, it now appears possible to accept that knowing and communicating through *narrative* is a secondary stage in the ontological (or coming to know and be known) process. The first phase of coming to know may indeed be a pre-reflective, pre-theorising, and pre-organising phase based on the process of creating and sharing stories. The second phase may then be a narrativising phase where stories are organised to mean something beyond the story itself, we tell the narrative when the dust has settled and we can retell the experience as a whole unit complete with our interpretation of what it meant/means.

The story is the 'now', the present telling in present tense,
jumbled, messy, vivid and happening, story is today;
But once slept on, tidied up, like socks rolled into a pair, stories-that-once-were transform into narratives
narratives speak of before, from the vantage of the now.

THE 'WHAT' OF THE STORIES OF WOMEN CASUAL ACADEMICS, AND THE 'HOW' OF THEIR IMPACT ON AN AUDIENCE

I also 'slept on' the stories women casual academics shared with me, 12 months of bits here and there shared through unstructured interviews, phone conversations and emails, and rolled them into a narrative consisting of six scenes of verbatim drama. But that was yesteryear and I've since presented the drama at several academic conferences, as both live performance and filmed drama, and listened with interest to audiences' formal and informal response and questions. My re-view of both the content and form of the narrative of the lived experience of women casual academics is therefore informed by the audiences' engagement with the dramatised narrative.

The drama was initially performed in 2015 within a university research conference at the University of the Sunshine Coast, Queensland, populated with approximately 150 casual academics and academics with ongoing employment, each of whom were formally invited to provide details of their engagement with the drama through a survey containing some closed but mainly open questions. I briefly share the main survey responses as they illuminate not what I aimed for (as has been the focus of the previous 6 chapters) but what was achieved in re-presenting a dramatised re-presentation of the lived experience of women casual academics.

When asked how they engaged with the performed data the vast majority of survey respondents (22 out of 27) identified that the narrative resonated strongly with them, or that it felt 'authentic' to them. More specifically, respondents claimed: "There was a clarity and authenticity which resonated deeply with me", 'Brave, revealing and all true'; "I related completely with the women", and "We all spoke afterwards and agreed that we felt as though you'd gotten the dialogue directly from us".

In addition, over two-thirds of respondents suggested that that their engagement with the performance was emotional: 'Emotion was the key, as some elements stuck without opportunity for release', 'I felt moved by the stories and surprised by the depth of their pain', and [it} 'provided a space to explore the emotive aspects and to humanise the stories'. Interesting, 15 respondents identified that their emotional response was physically experienced, with almost a third of respondents (8) advising that they had cried or been close to tears during the performance, 'Some sections were so close to home that it brought me to tears', 'I related completely with the women in the drama. I actually cried a few times. It was very raw and emotive', 'I had to fight back tears as I heard one after the other of my fears and frustrations voiced' and 'It made me cry to think we treat these intelligent strong women as if they are almost worthless'. Other corporeal reactions included, 'I felt it in my gut', and 'I don't think I moved for the whole show and the drama has stayed with me since'.

Yet, the emotional engagement of the audience did not appear to undermine a cognitive engagement with the narrative, or its lasting impact. For instance, respondents commented, 'It was emotive and intellectual', 'I think the drama was a powerful force that forced us to engage our hearts and minds and drew out a humane response', and 'compellingly emotive and intellectual', and 'It triggered lots of inner emotions which left me thinking about the drama for days afterwards – replaying aspects in my head', 'I thought about the drama a lot and it sparked debate and discussion for days', and 'it was compelling to watch and engaged all my senses and has stayed with me since'.

The survey respondents also commented on how the dramatic form of the re-presentation supported their engagement in the stories of women causal academics, and identified the political potency of drama: 'The only way to improve conditions for sessional academics is to find ways to increase understanding and empathy: not meaning to draw crude analogies but this is similar to the way documentaries can save whales; film and drama can plant a seed for social change', 'the lived experiences came to life because the actors made them 'real', Research data in written form would not have generated empathy to this extent', 'the dramatic representation made the stories more poignant, and the use of humour in parts made it permissible to challenge perceived authority', 'It was a very useful way to present the research – to provide voice of a large group that are muted'. In addition to the survey respondents' views, one of the women research participants who had contributed her story to the drama but did not complete a survey, emailed to me her thoughts on the impact of the performance:

> It was simply amazing. Hearing my story – and the story of thousands of other sessionals ... made me think of how court jesters and political cartoons have been used in the past to deliver difficult messages. Presenting what we have always been far too frightened to express ourselves

As only 18% of audience members completed a survey to identify response on how they engaged with the re-presentation of the lived experience of casual academics the findings can't be recognised as reflecting the audience population, but the comments from an audience created a unique opportunity for peer review (as audience feedback can be used to validate, critique or even trouble the research findings presented through non-traditional form/s). What was striking (to me) about the audience responses was their recognition of the impact of stories on their engagement and empathy; in line with Bruner's (1990) understanding, they identified the capacity of narrative to encompass rich descriptions of character, emotion, context and action which help to stimulate a sense of empathy. They also seemed to acknowledge the affordance of drama to 'open our senses' to others (Sikes and Gale 2006, chap. 2), and the role of fully embodied re-presentation in stimulating a physically affective response. Such a tendency to physically respond to a performed drama supports the notion that human beings primarily connect with others through a feeling of body (Wojciehowski and Gallese 2011) and that empathy is the outcome of 'our natural tendency to experience interpersonal relations first and foremost at the implicit level of intercorporeity' (Wojciehowski and Gallese 2011, 17). This appreciation of one's physical response to a performed narrative aligns with the feminist acceptance and celebration of the extra-rational knowing of lived experience, and endorses the capacity of arts-informed research to not only describe fully embodied lived experience, but to stimulate it. Finally, respondents also seemed to recognise the political and pollicising potential of verbatim drama to 'give voice to the voiceless' in society (Heddon 2008, 128), 'faceness' to the faceless (Wake 2013), or 'listening ears to the voices that often go unheard' (Wake 2010, 3). Therefore, the audience seemed to support the idea that 'the performance text is the single, most powerful tool for researchers to recover multiple meanings of lived experience' (Denzin 1997, 95) and so the medium of communication we use for our research needs to be central to both research planning and practice, and should not therefore be tagged on or considered as a post-research afterthought.

In addition to the initial performance of the drama based on the lived experience of women casual academics at a research conference, and on which the audience survey response was based, I also presented the filmed drama at The National Tertiary Education Union Insecure Work Conference, University of Tasmania, Australia; within a keynote address at the Benchmarking leadership and advancement of standards for sessional teaching (BLASST) National Summit, National Office of Learning and Teaching, Macquarie University, Sydney, and as part of panel discussion on Leading quality learning and teaching with sessional, casual or adjunct teachers at the 12th International Society for the Scholarship of Teaching and Learning Annual Conference, Melbourne. Whilst listening and responding to questions and comments at these conferences it struck me that two of the main preoccupations identified in stories of lived experience of women casual academics seemed to resonate deeply with both survey respondents and a significant number of the conference participants; most of whom were seeking recommendations for affecting change to the recruitment of casual academics in Australia. I therefore briefly *re*-view how the survey respondents describe/d their fear of unemployment/underemployment and the staff they perceive as responsible for work opportunities, and offer some suggestions for changes in recruitment policy.

When asked if they identified with a character or preoccupation presented in the drama, a half of survey respondents identified that they too experienced 'the uncertainty of employment', 'insecurity of continued work', 'lack of security', 'no job security', 'lack of consistency'; "The unknown – waiting for another contract, wondering if you are good enough, wondering what your income is going to be...' and that "It is disconcerting to know there is no continuity or certainty of employment or remuneration. I think many senior academics fail to realise this is a primary form of income for many people'.

Some respondents, and subsequent conference attendees, also suggested that fear of unemployment and the staff who employ them keep casual academics silence/d, "I believe the performance particularly and accurately portrayed the way women casual academics are practically muted. For fear of not getting any further work, many of us have been in unacceptable situations where we feel we cannot formally say anything or complain.', 'I learnt not to ask ... Feedback on teaching or the course was not tolerated', 'I was told "I'm the course coordinator and you're a tutor and I don't care what you think"', 'so it's best to keep your mouth shut". A few respondents more explicitly stated their fear of permanent staff, 'I was constantly terrified of Heads of School & Course Coordinators'.

This 'feedback from the coalface' (Brown, et al. 2010) resonates with Harvey and Fredericks' (2015) identification that very few instances of formalised policies or practices that support the recruitment or support of casual academics within the academy. So, informed by the stories shared to me by six women casual academics and the countless audience members and conference presenters over the last 18 months, it appears that much of the fear and anxiety around casualisation would be mitigated if the recruitment of casual academics was undertaken by a centralised Human Resources (HR) unit – in consultation with subject/unit coordinators. Where subject/course coordinators possess disciplinary and pedagogical content knowledge required to engage appropriately qualified and experience personnel, central HR units could ensure that offers of work to casual academics are de-personalised, professionally conducted, and that fair and equitable processes of recruitment take place. Thus, centralising the recruitment process might also make it easier for institutions to manage casual academics, maintain up to date records of their qualifications and experience, and both let them know of any ongoing work opportunities in their discipline or field and promote the casual academic to an interview panel were they to be shirt-listed for a permanent position. The process could also support year-long recruitment processes, instead of 10 or 13-week terms of employment to which most casual academics are subject. Of course, ideally, I would prefer for greater funding for Higher

Education and a reversal of the trend to casualisation, however, in the short term whilst Higher Education is operating in a funding starved neo liberalist culture, centralising recruitment for casual academics could at least protect casual staff from personalised ad-hoc and very short-term recruitment which layer fear and doubt onto their precarious experience.

A second outcome of the process of eliciting in/formal feedback from audiences not only allowed me to know what *they* deem/ed important or resonant in the drama, but when an audience are invited – and motivated – to share their lived experience of research outcomes they become transformed from being *receivers* of academic research to *active participants* in the project. And if we as researchers are open to a second set of narratives from audiences, then the shape and dynamic of the research process is changes to a participatory action research process, which further democratises the research process and more people are afforded an opportunity of voice.

Overall Reflections on the Process of Theatricalising the Lived Experience of Women Casual Academics

As I wanted to create listening ears for yet to be voiced women casual academics I needed to use a communication form that resists traditional academic discourse loaded with jargon and prohibitive language which renders it inaccessible to most of society – including those who in/directly fund the research or on whom the research is based (Carrigan 2017). I also wished to use a form of re-presentation that is congruent with the storied nature and individual experience of all participants' experience. I decided therefore to employ polyphonic drama that allows several individual stories to be placed alongside each other, in equal value with one another, without 'protagonistic' privilege. I was additionally motivated to use a form of communication to reflect and inhabit the fully embodied, imagistic, and dynamic nature of lived experience. In response, I employed a proto-verbatim theatre performance which centralises the words and imbedded paralinguistic meaning of participants' fully stories, whilst simultaneously incorporating my engagement with and refraction of the women's stories, in the re-presentation. I also solicited audience's response to the performed drama to further democratise the research design and allow the research to transform from an arts-inform narrative inquiry to a participatory action-research process where the original participants, myself as story gatherer, and the audience, were provided with an opportunity to share our experiences of the casualisation of academia.

Through the process I learn/ed to be unafraid of letting the research journey unfold, of taking pit stops to check that the direction of the research journey is in alignment with the main aims of the project, and in doing so I encounter/ed new ideas, affects, and scholarship along the way. I also learn/ed to de-throne the masculine traditional of linearity and a priori and revel/led in the merging of feminist 'promiscuous' and 'yet to be named' (Childers et al. 2013) practices with more traditional research processes. For instance, I elicited stories through narrative inquiry, re-storeyed them using established holistic *and* affectively-driven processes, re-presented them through a drama performance, and weaved audience's experience with participants' stories to create recommendations. Finally, one of the main preoccupations and practices of the project was the fluid amalgamations of masculine with feminine or bicultural (Blankenship and Robson 1995) forms of communication.

I was not only compelled to re-present the voices of women casual academics in a form congruent with their content and accessible for a wide audience, but was motivated by an understanding more broadly that stories of the yet to be voiced, *in form and content,* need to be re-presented. I extend Rindfleish et al.'s (2009) appeal for 'more stories need to be heard in openly public spaces for there to be some recognition of the ongoing disadvantage women experience in academia' (Rindfleish et al. 2009, 487), by suggesting that the stories of ongoing disadvantage need to be presented in a form that disrupts the hegemony that traditional academic structures inhabit and propagate. And I expand Boje's (1995) request that we celebrate a multiplicity of stories and storytellers within academic organisations, by finding a multiplicity *of forms* through which to tell our stories. I thus stand with brave and sassy women scholars who show us 'other ways' of doing academic work, and who remind us that 'the very words we speak and the grammatical structures we use actually influence or determine the way we think. In this light, language is not just a means of communicating ideas, it actually helps fashion them' (Open University 1981, 72).

Therefore, in concert with Lorde I accept that 'the master's tools will never dismantle the master's house' (1981), and so we need Other forms to accommodate Other/s' ideas; and I cheer Morley (2016) when she suggests that we use our 'academic creativity to incorporate transgression and re-signification, and not just compliance and mechanistic productivity' (p. 40). I also applaud Barad (2010) who reminds us that 'we inherit the future, not just the past', and so need to inhabit and create a new imaginary which includes form and substance. So, like 'Socratic 'gadflies' unsettling and critiquing academic practices that are prescriptive, restrictive, reductive, and masculine, that refuse oxygen to the lives of Other subjects, let's embrace forms that afford us opportunity to speak, to paint or to dance our (often Othered) truth. And I finally invite you to stand with me as I stand with Cixous when she sings

> Woman must write herself: must write about women and bring women to writing, from which they have been driven away as violently as from their bodies-for the same reasons, by the same law, with the same fatal goal. Woman must put herself into the text-as into the world and into history-by her own movement. (Cixous 1976, 875)

Through the arts, and theatre more specifically, we can write and show our stories, and hear and tell the stories of Others. Be not quiet or still, for if you write not yourself, someone else will write/right it for you, and it may very well be written in a form unintelligible to you, and Others like you.

References

Barad, K. (2010). Quantum Entanglements and Hauntological Relations of Inheritance: Dis/Continuities, Spacetime Enfoldings, and Justice-to-Come. *Derrida Today, 3*(2), 240–268. https://doi.org/10.3366/E1754850010000813

Blankenship, J., & Robson, D. C. (1995). A 'Feminine Style'; in Women's Political Discourse: An Exploratory Essay. *Communication Quarterly, 43*(3), 353–366. https://doi.org/10.1080/01463379509369982

Bloomberg, L. D., & Volpe, M. (2012). *Completing Your Qualitative Dissertation: A Road Map from Beginning to End.* Thousand Oaks: Sage.

Blumenreich, M. (2004). Avoiding the Pitfalls of 'Conventional' Narrative Research: Using Poststructural Theory to Guide the Creation of Narratives of Children with HIV. *Qualitative Research, 4*(1), 77–90. https://doi.org/10.1177/1468794104041108

Boje, D. M. (1995). Stories of the Storytelling Organization: A Postmodern Analysis of Disney as "Tamara-Land". *The Academy of Management Journal, 38*(4), 997–1035. https://doi.org/10.2307/256618

Boje, D. M. (2001). *Narrative Methods for Organizational and Communication Research.* Thousand Oaks: Sage.

Brown, T., Goodman, J., & Yasukawa, K. (2010). Academic Casualization in Australia: Class Divisions in the University. *Journal of Industrial Relations*, 52(2), 169–182. https://doi.org/10.1177/0022185609359443

Bruner, J. S. (1990). *Acts of Meaning*. Cambridge: Harvard University Press.

Carrigan, M. (2017). An Interview with Patricia Leavy About Research Design in Contemporary Times. *The Sociological Imagination*. http://sociologicalimagination.org/archives/19315. Accessed 8 May 2017.

Childers, S. M., Rhee, J.-E., & Daza, S. L. (2013). Promiscuous (Use of) Feminist Methodologies: The Dirty Theory and Messy Practice of Educational Research Beyond Gender. *International Journal of Qualitative Studies in Education*, 26(5), 507–523. https://doi.org/10.1080/09518398.2013.786849

Cixous, H. (1976). The Laugh of the Medusa. *Signs*, 1(4), 875–893. http://www.jstor.org/stable/3173239

Clandinin, D. J., & Connelly, F. M. (2000). *Narrative inquiry: Experience and story in qualitative research*. San Francisco: Jossey-Bass.

Denzin, N. K. (1997). Performance Texts. In W. G. Tierney & Y. S. Lincoln (Eds.), *Representation and the Text: Re-framing the Narrative Voice* (pp. 179–217). Albany: State University of New York Press.

Harvey, M., & Fredericks, V. (2015). *Quality Learning and Teaching with Sessional Staff, Herdsa Guide*. Milperra: HERDSA.

Heddon, D. (2008). *Autobiography and Performance*. Basingstoke: Palgrave Macmillan.

Lorde, A. (1981). The Master's Tools Will Never Dismantle the Master's House. In C. Morraga & G. Anzaldua (Eds.), *This Bridge Called My Back: Writing by Radical Women* (pp. 98–101). Watertown: Persephone Press.

Morley, L. (2016). Troubling Intra-Actions: Gender, Neo-liberalism and Research in the Global Academy. *Journal of Education Policy*, 31(1), 28–45. https://doi.org/10.1080/02680939.2015.1062919

Neilsen, L. (2002). Learning from the Liminal: Fiction as Knowledge. *Alberta Journal of Education Research*, 48(3), 206–214. http://ajer.journalhosting.ucalgary.ca/index.php/ajer/article/viewFile/326/318. Accessed 28 Sept 2017.

Open University. (1981). *Book 2: Social Aspects of Language in E263, Language in Use*. Milton Keynes: Open University Press.

Rindfleish, J., Sheridan, A., & Kjeldal, S.-E. (2009). Creating an "Agora" for Storytelling as a Way of Challenging the Gendered Structures of Academia. *Equal Opportunities International*, 28(6), 486–499. https://doi.org/doi:10.1108/02610150910980783

Scott-Maxwell, F. (1979). *The Measure of My Days* (1st ed.). New York: Penguin Books.

Sikes, P., & Gale, K. (2006). *Narrative Approaches to Education Research*. Plymouth: Faculty of Education, University of Plymouth.

Wake, C. (2010). Towards a Working Definition of Verbatim Theatre. In P. Brown (Ed.), *Verbatim: Staging Memory and Community* (pp. 2–5). Strawberry Hills: Currency Press.

Wake, C. (2013). To Witness Mimesis: The Politics, Ethics, and Aesthetics of Testimonial Theatre in through the Wire 1. *Modern Drama, 56*(1), 102–125. https://doi.org/10.1353/mdr.2013.0009

Wojciehowski, H., & Gallese, V. (2011). How Stories Make Us Feel: Toward an Embodied Narratology. *California Italian Studies, 2*(1), 1–38. http://www.escholarship.org/uc/item/3jg726c2

INDEX

A
AnOther, 13, 49
Arts-informed research, 28–32, 66, 83, 84, 88, 109

B
Barthes, Roland Gérard, 8
Belenky, Mary Field, 6, 17, 30
Bicultural communication, 22, 23, 112
Bruner, Jerome S., 8, 28, 96, 108

C
Casual academics, 1–9, 15–17, 45–47
Casualisation, 2, 5–9, 110, 111
Cixous, Hélène, 19–22, 82, 113

E
Écriture feminine, 19, 20, 81
Elephant(s) in the room, 2–9
Emotions, 6, 7, 15–21, 23, 31–33, 37–40

F
Feminine ways of communicating, 19–20
Feminine ways of knowing, 17–19, 30
Feminism, 22
Feminist methodology, 33–35
Feminist research, 29–30
Feminist theatre, 55

G
Gilligan, Carol, 18, 30
Grapholect, 15–16

H
Hardy, Barbara, 7, 8, 28

L
Langer, Susanne, 21–22
Lived experience, 24, 27–32, 101

© The Author(s) 2018   117
G. Crimmins, *Theatricalising Narrative Research on Women Casual Academics*, Palgrave Studies in Gender and Education, https://doi.org/10.1007/978-3-319-71562-9

M
Masculine methodology, 2, 4, 15–17, 23, 24
Measure, 4–7, 46

N
Narrative enquiry, 21, 28–34, 37–40, 46–54, 103
Neoliberalism, 110–111

O
Othering, 14, 16
Others, 14, 96, 107, 111

P
Proto-verbatim theatre, 59, 83–85, 97

R
Researcher role, 21, 63–66, 81–84, 97
Restorying, 81–85

Richardson, Laurel, 21, 22, 30, 49, 65, 66, 86

S
Scholartist, 82, 96
Self-narration, 8
Silence, 16, 22, 23, 37, 46, 51, 89, 110
Speaking, 14, 16, 46–49, 105
Spivak, Gayatri Chakravorty, 16–17
Storytelling, 105

T
Theatricalising, 39, 52, 58, 83, 101–104, 111

V
Verbatim drama, 47–54, 58, 63–66
Voice, 9, 13–17, 21, 27–33, 36
Voicelessness, 9, 13–17, 22

Printed by Printforce, the Netherlands